My
Evernote®

Katherine Murray

800 East 96th Street,
Indianapolis, Indiana 46240 USA

My Evernote®

Trademarks

Warning and Disclaimer

Bulk Sales

Que Publishing offers excellent discounts on this book when ordered in quantity for bulk purchases or special sales. For more information, please contact

U.S. Corporate and Government Sales

1-800-382-3419

corpsales@pearsontechgroup.com

For sales outside the United States, please contact

International Sales

international@pearson.com

EDITOR-IN-CHIEF
Greg Wiegand

EXECUTIVE EDITOR
Loretta Yates

DEVELOPMENT EDITOR
Todd Brakke

MANAGING EDITOR
Sandra Schroeder

SENIOR PROJECT EDITOR
Tonya Simpson

COPY EDITOR
Paula Lowell

INDEXER
Cheryl Lenser

PROOFREADER
Kathy Ruiz

TECHNICAL EDITOR
James Kelly

PUBLISHING
COORDINATOR
Cindy Teeters

BOOK DESIGNER
Anne Jones

COMPOSITOR
Bronkella Publishing

Contents at a Glance

Table of Contents

3   **Capturing and Tagging Your First Notes** **55**

About the Author

Katherine Murray has been writing about technology since the early 1980s (no joke!) and loves writing about technology that connects. She's an avid researcher and has filled notebook after notebook (after *notebook*!) with clips, quotes, and snippets from books and sites she finds interesting. Katherine finds Evernote exciting because its inclusive, cross-platform, and flexible approach makes it a great app with worldwide appeal. In addition to writing books, Katherine writes regularly for CNET's TechRepublic, Windows Secrets, and the PC World Business Center. You can contact Katherine through her blogs, BlogOffice and Connect & Coblogerate, or by following her on Twitter at @kmurray230.

Dedication

I dedicate this book to the idea lovers, the project designers, the creative artists, the puzzling scientists, the geeky gadget developers, and the never-say-die tech enthusiasts who want a great way to collect—and later, find—the terrific ideas that bubble up during the course of the day.

Acknowledgments

You've probably heard it said that writing is a solitary effort, and I suppose that's true, to a point. While I'm writing the paragraphs you read here, I'm sitting at my desk, with only my cat Maya for company. But after I finish writing, a whole group of people have a part in making the book as good as it can be. And this collaboration is one of my favorite parts of the whole process.

Many thanks to the entire group at Que Publishing for their vision, excitement, support, and great editing all the way through *My Evernote*. Special thanks as always to Loretta Yates for thinking of me for this book, and to Todd Brakke, book developer; Paula Lowell, copy editor; and James Kelly, technical editor—who each helped to ensure that this book is as accurate as possible and the examples and tasks are easy to read and follow.

We Want to Hear from You!

As the reader of this book, *you* are our most important critic and commentator. We value your opinion and want to know what we're doing right, what we could do better, what areas you'd like to see us publish in, and any other words of wisdom you're willing to pass our way.

As an editor-in-chief for Que Publishing, I welcome your comments. You can email or write me directly to let me know what you did or didn't like about this book—as well as what we can do to make our books better.

Please note that I cannot help you with technical problems related to the topic of this book. We do have a User Services group, however, where I will forward specific technical questions related to the book.

When you write, please be sure to include this book's title and author as well as your name, email address, and phone number. I will carefully review your comments and share them with the author and editors who worked on the book.

Email: feedback@quepublishing.com

Mail: Greg Wiegand
Editor-in-Chief
Que Publishing
800 East 96th Street
Indianapolis, IN 46240 USA

Reader Services

Visit our website and register this book at quepublishing.com/register for convenient access to any updates, downloads, or errata that might be available for this book.

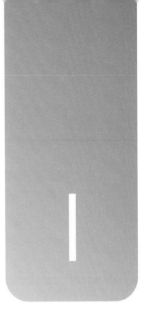

Introduction

What inspires you? Are you always finding information that you want to save somewhere, scribble down, or sketch and keep for later? Are you fascinated with mobile phones, searching for just the right new house, looking to build a garden shed, or trying to organize a big research project?

Do you collaborate with a team—of teachers, salespeople, editors, or family members?

Do you want a way to capture and organize all the inspiring bits you bump into, whether you're using a PC, Mac, phone, or other device?

If your answer to any of these questions is "yes," you're going to love Evernote!

Evernote is a wildly popular digital note-taking application that has more than 10 million users worldwide. The free application is available just about anywhere—and can be used in just about any way—you want to take notes. You can create and update your Evernote notebooks on the Web, and then add to them when you're working at your PC, checking in with your tablet, browsing the Web, or using your phone.

In this book you'll learn how to use Evernote to capture and arrange all those great ideas you think of or things you discover throughout your day and organize them in a way in which you can find them easily later. What's more, you'll learn how to use Evernote on a variety of devices to capture notes in all kinds of formats. You can also share your notebooks—while keeping your notes secure—to make collaboration across all devices simple and clean.

Highlights of Evernote

If you think about it for a minute, you can probably come up with several characteristics you would like a note-taking program to have, including the following:

- It needs to be fast and easy to use.

- It needs to be flexible so that you can add notes quickly when you think of them and not have to jump through a number of hoops to record a single note in a notebook.

- It needs to work with a variety of platforms so that you can add notes wherever you are.

What if you could combine all these features—and have them for free? Yes, you guessed it—that's Evernote.

Include text,
Add tags   images,
Save your notes in a notebook   to notes   and voice

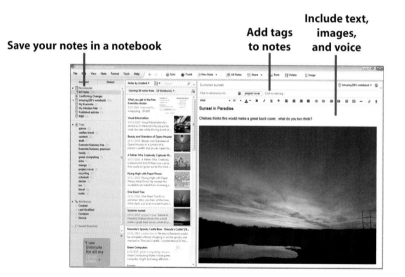

Evernote combines a number of features that make capturing and organizing information easy and fast. For example, you can

- **Capture your notes** in the format that fits them best—text, pictures, audio, or web clippings

- **Scan items directly into Evernote** using a scanner that can save directly to the program or by setting up your scanner to email scanned images to your Evernote account

- **Save your notes** in an online notebook that syncs automatically with the notebook on your PC, Mac, or mobile device

- **Store items you use often**—forms, checklists, plans, itineraries—in your Evernote notebook so that you can always find them easily

- **Tag your notes** using tags you design so that you can easily find information you need later

- **Share your notes** with others and collaborate securely on projects

- **Find inspiration** in the creative and vibrant Evernote community

- **Discover extra apps** in the Evernote Trunk that you can use to extend your note-taking talents

You'll find all these features covered throughout this book in the appropriate chapters, with tips and sidebars to add to your practice and understanding of Evernote.

Versions of Evernote

In the three short years since 2008, when Evernote first launched as an open beta, the program has skyrocketed to a worldwide audience of more than 10 million users. In fact, since those early days when CEO Phil Libin posted on the Evernote blog that they "watched with equal parts glee and horror" as the number of beta users climbed to 50,000, the program has spiraled through numerous updates and announcements for computers and devices of all sorts.

One of the great things about Evernote is that, thanks to the creative and industrious development team, the various versions are continually updated so that you're always getting the most current Evernote features available. Every few months (or weeks!) new releases are made available for the Mac, iOS, BlackBerry, Android, Windows Phone, or Windows PC versions. And on top of that, Evernote continues to add new tools, such as Skitch, Evernote Hello, Evernote Food, Evernote Clearly, and Evernote Peek. (Don't worry; you'll hear more about these tools later in the book.)

One of the challenges in writing about a quickly evolving program like Evernote is that you might notice that the screens you see are slightly different from the illustrations in the book. This happens because Evernote will continue to tweak things long after this book appears on bookstore shelves. Rest assured, however, that we've captured the basic functionality of the program here, and even if your screen looks a little different down the road, you will always be able to capture, organize, and share your great ideas in Evernote!

In addition to all these versions of Evernote—as though that's not enough—Evernote also comes in both free and premium versions. Chances are that you can do much of what you want to do using the Evernote free version; at least, it may be the place to begin. If you decide you want to upgrade to the premium version (for only $5 per month or $45 per year), you get additional functionality such as super-sizing your uploads, editing collaboratively on shared notebooks, increased number of emails per month in which you can email notes to your Evernote notebooks, and a shortcut to the front of the tech support line.

It's Okay to Think About It a While

You'll have a chance to weigh out the benefits of upgrading to the premium version in Chapter 1, "Getting Started with Evernote." This book covers both versions, so you won't be left out in the cold no matter which version you choose.

Extra Features in *My Evernote*

My Evernote uses an inviting, visual format to teach you the basics of getting the most from the Evernote notebooks you create and use. Images in the book show you how to master beginning to intermediate Evernote tasks quickly; the numbers on the illustrations show you what to do next and the corresponding text explains the steps involved.

In addition to the tutorial text in the chapters, you'll find a number of extra features to help you expand what you learn and try in Evernote. Tips highlight shortcuts and workarounds in the program; Go Further sidebars provide additional information about techniques you may want to research or try on your own; and It's Not All Good sidebars point out potential trouble spots and unexpected glitches so that you can avoid getting stuck in the same issues your author stumbled into.

Because Evernote works with all the major PC models and popular devices (including Windows PCs, Macs, iPhones, Androids, BlackBerrys, iPads, and Windows Phone 7), you'll find that this book includes Evernote ideas you can use with these different platforms. In fact, we've added icons to help you see at a glance where an Evernote feature is related to a specific computer or device:

 This icon highlights a feature that is available only on Windows computers and devices.

 This icon shows you that the feature is available only for Apple iOS systems and devices.

This icon lets you know that a specific feature is available only for mobile devices or tablets (and the text will let you know to which devices the text refers).

What You'll Find in This Book

Evernote is fun and creative. So this book takes a high-energy, creative, you-can-do-it approach to the most important tasks you need as you gather up your great ideas and do something with them in Evernote. You'll find out how to create a new notebook and add notes in all sorts of ways, embellishing them to your heart's desire with images, voice notes, handwriting, and more. You'll learn to share notes and notebooks in various ways and add to your

Evernote experience so that it works just the way you want it to. Specifically here's what you'll find:

- Chapter 1, "Getting Started with Evernote," introduces you to the basics of the program and shows you how to create an Evernote account and download Evernote for your Windows computer or mobile device. You'll also find out about setting your account preferences and learn about the basic tools you'll use in the Evernote window.

- Chapter 2, "Evernote Everywhere, on Everything!," shows you how to install Evernote on your Windows PC or device, Mac, iPad, or Android. You'll learn about features unique to the Windows, Apple, and Android versions of Evernote and find out about synchronizing your notes across multiple devices.

- Chapter 3, "Capturing and Tagging Your First Notes," introduces you to creating a new note, complete with title, source, and tags. You'll learn how to add notes directly from your Twitter or Google+ accounts, and paste note content from other sources.

- Chapter 4, "Editing and Formatting Notes," helps you edit note content and change the font, size, and style of text. You'll also find out how to change the text color, alter the format (for example, creating bulleted and numbered lists), and add to-do lists with checkboxes. In this chapter you'll also discover how to rename and delete notes you no longer need.

- Chapter 5, "Adding and Working with Images," takes a close look at adding pictures to your Evernote notebooks. Here you'll learn how to paste pictures, import images, resize and edit photos, and save a picture for use outside of your notebook.

- Chapter 6, "Inking Your Notes," begins by exploring the various inking features in Evernote. You will find out how to create an ink note, change your pen, select the line style and color, and undo and redo your inked note.

- Chapter 7, "Grabbing Web Clippings and Webcam Notes," gives you the freedom to browse to the sites that fascinate you and grab the notes you want to add to your Evernote notebook. You'll also find out how to create webcam notes and share those notes with others.

- Chapter 8, "Recording Audio Notes," enables you to listen to your inner and outer voices by capturing your thoughts in audio format. This chapter shows you how to set up audio, record your notes, add the notes to your notebook, and work with the notes you've added.

- Chapter 9, "Creating and Managing Notebooks" shows you how you can organize your notes into specific notebooks so that you collect information in the way that makes the most sense to you. You'll learn how to create a new notebook, create an offline notebook, synchronize your notebooks, move notes around, work with notebook stacks, secure your notebooks, and import notebooks from other programs.

- Chapter 10, "Finding and Viewing Notes Your Way," shows you how to search for notes using note attributes and tags. You'll also find out how to create and use saved searches, change Evernote views, rearrange and reorder notes, and hide and display notes.

- Chapter 11, "Previewing and Printing Your Notes," is about all things printing in regard to your Evernote notebooks. Learn how to view a note in Print Preview, change the notes pages you want to see, magnify your notes, set printer options, and print the notes you want.

- Chapter 12, "Sharing Notes with Others," shows you how to share the notebooks you create while keeping them secure both online and offline. Learn how to share your notebook with individuals or make your notebook public. You can also email notes or explore notes and notebooks to share with others.

The chapters are organized so that you can jump in and read about whatever interests you most, or you can choose to go through the book sequentially if you like.

Along the way, you'll find extra information to help you get the most of Evernote, whether you're working with your PC or Mac, web browser, or mobile device.

Let's Begin

If you're tired of losing those napkins, sticky tabs, and scraps of paper that have important information written on them, it's time to begin using Evernote. Getting started is simple, and because the program makes setting up your notes and notebooks in the way that makes the most sense to you easy, the approach is flexible. You can add items as you go and use only what you need today.

Sounds simple, right? Let's get started by creating an Evernote account, downloading the program, and taking a look around. The next chapter shows you how to create an Evernote account and download the program. Chapter 2 walks you through installing Evernote on Windows, Mac, and mobile devices and gives you a tour of the Evernote window.

So when you're ready, turn the page to get started on your path to creative note-taking with Evernote.

Create your first
notebook in a
matter of minutes

Add notes easily using
Evernote on your phone

With Evernote, you can capture, organize, and share all kinds of notes you create— using the web, your PC, or your phone. In this chapter, you prepare for note-taking goodness by completing the following tasks:

→ Envisioning How You'll Use Evernote

→ Creating Your Evernote Account

→ Setting Your Account Preferences

→ Exploring Evernote on the Web

→ Downloading Evernote

Getting Started with Evernote

One of the great things about Evernote is that you can use it in just about any way that makes sense to you. That means it will fit your own particular creative style, no questions asked. You don't have to worry about learning some method of organizing your thoughts that doesn't particularly connect with your way of doing things. If you're a visual learner, for example, you may be drawn to beautiful images, smart diagrams, and effective tables that you find online or that you find displayed in the world.

You start out with a blank canvas, and you can either add all sorts of notes in no particular order, or design an elaborate system of notebooks and file notes as you go. What's more, you can move seamlessly from your PC or Mac, your phone or other mobile device, or your web browser, and Evernote syncs your notes no matter where you enter them, so you're always looking at the most current notes, no matter where you are.

In this chapter, you learn to create an Evernote account, start your first notebook online, explore the web tools Evernote offers, and download Evernote to your computer or mobile device.

How Will You Use Evernote?

Part of the great appeal of Evernote is its flexibility. Instead of insisting that you capture, organize, and file your notes in a particular way, Evernote's open structure makes taking notes and arranging them in the way that fits your style best easy. For example, you might want to use Evernote in the following ways:

- Gather information you need for a project you're starting

- Create a space where you can share information with friends who are planning a party

- Organize an online family cookbook

- Create a shared creative space for people in your small business to brainstorm about new products

- Design shared space online where your sales staff can access the latest news and company updates, and upload reports—using any platform (PC, web, or phone) they choose

Thinking It Through—or Not

Some people are planners and like to have some sense of how the tools they use fit into their everyday needs. Others are more fly-by-the-seat-of-their-pants types, preferring to create their notes and notebooks as they go. Whichever method suits you best, Evernote is flexible enough to give you what you need to capture, organize, and share your notes easily.

Me, Myself, and Evernote

If you plan to use Evernote to collect, organize, and use notes for projects you work on solo, you can keep your information secure in one easy-to-access and continually updated place. Evernote always syncs your notes with your web notebook, so you can easily add to your notes on the go and update them from any point you have access online. You can post notes from your phone, email ideas to your Evernote notebook, add audio notes, clip things from the web, and much more. Plus your notebooks sync automatically among all your devices—computer, phone, and web browser—so you're always working with your most current information, no matter how you access your notebooks.

You can easily post notes from your phone to your Evernote notebook

Tap to open a note

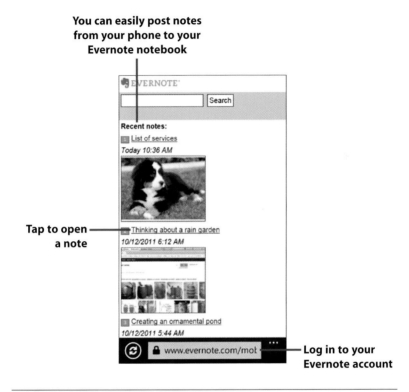

Log in to your Evernote account

Different Flavors of Evernote

Although Evernote is available—and fully functional—as a free application, users of Premium accounts have access to a number of additional features. If you pay $5 per month or $45 a year for a premium account, you have the ability to upload larger files, email yourself more notes per day (the limit is 50 for free users and 250 per day for Premium users), edit shared notebooks (as opposed to just viewing them), and view your Evernote notebooks with no promotional ads.

Evernote for Teams

Evernote offers teams a simple and secure way to brainstorm, share research, collect interesting designs and ideas, and work collaboratively on projects, whether team members use PCs or Macs, computers or phones, web browsers or tablets. The flexibility of the program really shines when you have multiple users all contributing to the same pool of information. You can easily search for notes by a specific person or that were posted from a particular source (for example, perhaps the notes were emailed to Evernote, posted from a phone, or clipped from a web page), and you can create saved searches so that you can find items you search for often in your Evernote notebook.

Share your notebook with others so you can collaborate easily

Add as many tags as you need to describe your content

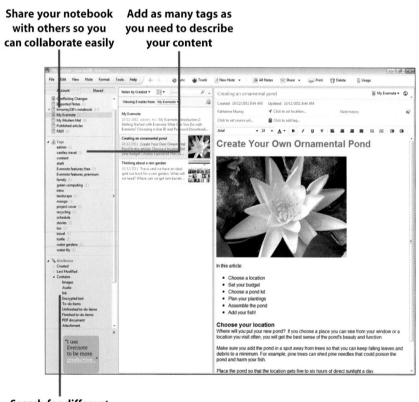

Search for different types of data

Evernote in the Classroom

Today, schools are—by necessity, some say—moving into the new online world for all kinds of student projects and possibilities. Think about it—creating a shared Evernote notebook for your class, or for groups within your class, gives your students a way to collaborate easily and naturally in an electronic domain that comes naturally to them (perhaps even more than it does to you!).

As the teacher, you can post the latest classroom notes, add assignment information, provide resources, and more. Students can read your latest postings, submit their assignments, ask questions, and work on collaborative research or creative projects of their own. The tool is as flexible as you need it to be and offers easy access (from a variety of computers and devices) and a secure environment for ongoing student work. You can even post your new notes to your school's Facebook account if you want to share your class ideas or events with a larger audience.

You can create multiple notebooks to organize work for different classes

Interact with your students in a shared notebook

Post notes to social media

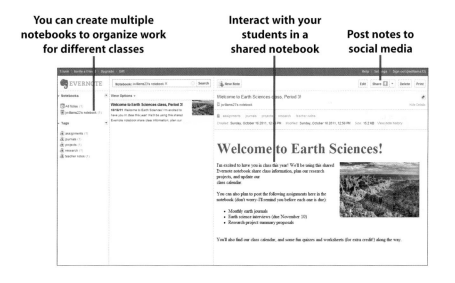

Evernote for Business

Evernote can help small businesses solve all kinds of information-and-people-management problems. Do you regularly collect reports from your salespeople in the field? Create a shared sales notebook in Evernote where your sales staff can upload their weekly reports. Does your business rely heavily on schedules that are always being updated? Post the latest information once in Evernote and all your team members will receive the updates automatically the next time they view your shared notebook on the web, on their computers, or by phone.

Tag your notes so that you can find them easily on any device

Your notes sync automatically to the web

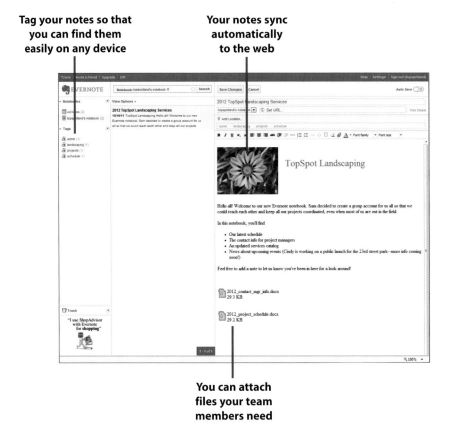

You can attach files your team members need

Erasing the Rules

Until recently, free account users could add only add text, pictures, audio, and PDF files to their notes but in summer 2011, that restriction was lifted. Now both free and premium users can attach literally any type of file to a note. Evernote says they changed the rule because "we want to allow our users to store everything related to an experience or memory in a single, visual, searchable place." Nice.

Evernote for Nonprofits

Nonprofit organizations are often characterized by their need for flexibility—unless you're part of a large organization, chances are that you wear many hats. You might write the newsletter, do the fundraising, and organize volunteers, all in the same week! Evernote makes it easy for you to share notebooks with your management team, post schedules and updates, post notes about upcoming events and needs for volunteers, and much more. You can easily create multiple notebooks—for example, one for management, one for volunteers, and one for storing your fundraising information. You can also apply different security measures for the notebooks so your volunteers can access the ones containing the information they need, while the management and fundraising notebooks are for management eyes only.

You can share notebooks with different groups of users

Switch among notebooks easily

Setting Up Your Evernote Account

As you've seen from the examples in this chapter, you can set up Evernote to work in a way that best fits your work style. Your first step is to create an Evernote account, and then you can create your first notebook on the web. Note that this step isn't necessary, however—part of the flexibility of Evernote is that you can download the app and install it on your computer or device and then create your first notebook in that way as well.

Creating Your Account

Your work begins on the Evernote home page, where you can create an account and access your first web notebook. Like everything else in Evernote, however, this process is flexible—you can download the app and install it and create your Evernote account after the fact, if you choose.

1. Go to www.evernote.com.

2. Click Web Sign In in the top-right corner of the window.

3. Click Create an Account. The Getting Started with Evernote window appears.

EVERNOTE®

Get started with Evernote

▸About Evernote ▸Blog

You're seconds away from having perfect memory!

Evernote is ready to collect all of your ideas, experiences, thoughts, and memories into an always-accessible place.

- Take down your inspirations and ideas as they happen
- Capture interesting webpages you see, images and all
- Snap photos of everything from whiteboards to wine labels

Then, find it all any time from your computer, phone, or the web!

Complete the registration form on this page to get started.

If you already have an account, please Sign in.

Did you forget your password?

Register for Evernote

Full name

Email address*

Username*

Password*

Confirm password*

☐ You accept our Terms of Service and confirm that you are at least 13 years old.

Word verification*   Type numbers you see in the picture below.

86365

• denotes required fields   Register

Downloads | Blog | Developers | Contact Us | Technical Support | Terms of Service | Privacy Policy   © 2011, Evernote Corporation.

4. Enter your name in the Full Name field.

5. Type your email address.

6. Enter a username. Evernote checks to make sure the name you entered is available.

7. Enter and confirm your password.

8. Read through and accept the Evernote terms of service. Service terms include much of what you'd expect to see—parameters about user conduct, rights, liabilities, and limitations.

9. Enter the verification code (to let Evernote know you are a real person creating a real account, as opposed to a spambot).

10. Click Register. Evernote sends a confirmation code to the email address you entered.

10. Check your email account for an email from the Evernote team that includes a confirmation code. Type the confirmation code in the Evernote window.

11. Click Confirm.

What's in a Name?

If the name you enter in the username field isn't available, Evernote displays the message *Username has already been taken*. If you want to stay as close to that name as possible, you can vary the name by adding a number following the name (for example, *katherine23*) or by adding a hyphen or an underscore in the name (such as *katherine_23*).

Logging in to Evernote

After you create your Evernote account, you can log in and start adding your notes on the web.

1. On the Welcome to Evernote screen, enter your password.

2. Click Sign In.

Signing in Next Time

You'll see the Welcome to Evernote screen only the first time you log in after signing up for a new account. When you return to Evernote on the web in the future, by going to www.evernote.com, you can simply click Web Sign In in the upper-right corner of the screen. You can then enter your username and password to access your Evernote account.

Exploring Evernote on the Web

After you log in using your Evernote username and password, the Welcome to Evernote window appears. Evernote creates the first note for you, offering suggestions and links to get you started. You can also check your account settings and get help while you are using the web version of Evernote.

Evernote—the Web Version

Using Evernote on the web, you can create a new notebook, add notes to the notebook, tag your notes, change the way your notes are displayed, and more. In fact, the features in the web version of Evernote are complete; you could use Evernote on the web without downloading the app to your computer, your phone, or your tablet, if you choose.

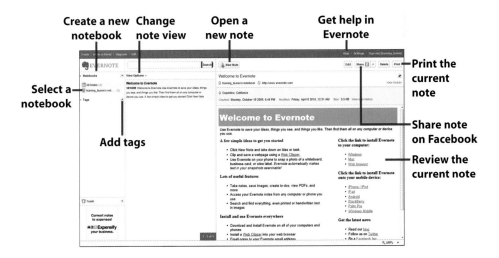

From Web to PC to Phone

Evernote is available in several different versions, each optimized to take advantage of the specific format for your PC or device. For example, you can use Evernote on your PC or Android phone, download it to your iPad 2, and use it on the web. This makes adding to your notebooks easy, whether you're in your office or on the road. Each version of Evernote looks a little different—for example, the phone version is configured for a small screen display, and you select options for notebooks and notes using a different process than you'll follow on the web. Later in this chapter you'll download Evernote for your computer or mobile device; in Chapter 2, you'll install Evernote and set it up to work the way you want it to on your computer and phone.

Reviewing Your Account Settings

You can view your Evernote account settings to see how much of your monthly note space you've used, how much longer remains in the monthly cycle, what type of account you're using, and how many web clippings, picture postings, audio notes, and photos you have available in your account.

1. Go to www.evernote.com in your browser window.
2. Click Web Sign In.

3. Enter your username if necessary.

4. Type your password.

5. Click Sign In.

6. Click Settings.

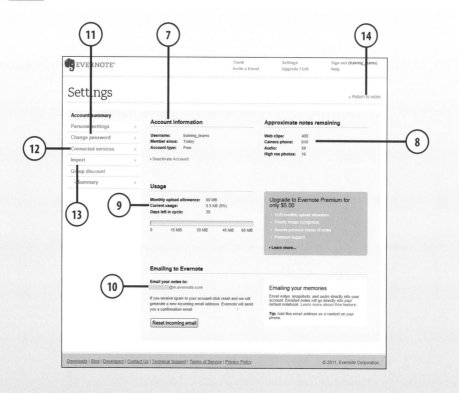

7. Review your account information and type.

8. Check the number and types of notes available to you. This information tells you the number of web clips, camera phone posts, audio notes, and photos you can still add to your notebook this month (the numbers here vary depending on which account type you use and how many notes you've already posted in the current month).

9. Check your monthly Evernote usage.

10. Get the email address for your Evernote account.

11. Change your password. On the next Settings window, enter your current password and type the new password; then retype the new one and click Change.

12. Connect Evernote to Facebook and Google, a topic I discuss in Chapter 12. In the Connected Services window, click the Connect button for either Facebook or Google (or both, one at a time) and then click Allow to enable Evernote to access your social media information, post to your account, and access your Facebook or Google data.

13. Import notebooks from Google Notebook. Enter a name for the notebook to which you want to import your Google Notebook data, and then click Browse to find the Google Atom Notebook file. Click Open and then Import Notes to import the Google notebook to Evernote.

14. Click Return to Notes to exit the Settings area and return to your notebook.

A Little Extra Help with the Google Notebook Importer

Evernote has posted a video clip on YouTube to show users how to import Google notebooks into Evernote. You'll find the clip on YouTube at www.youtube.com/user/EvernoteAndrew#p/u/51/dvJn7hOhbJ8.

Emailing Your Notes

On the Account Summary page in your Evernote Settings, you'll find the email address you can use to email your notes directly to your Evernote notebook. Simply add the email address displayed in the Emailing to Evernote area to the address book on your phone or mobile device and you'll be able to add notes directly to your default notebook by simply emailing them in. You learn more about emailing notes to your Evernote notebook in Chapter 3, "Capturing and Tagging Your First Notes."

Getting Help Online

Evernote is a simple program to use, but that doesn't mean you won't have questions while you use it. For that reason, developers built in a comprehensive help system that answers your questions and gives you access to tutorial video clips, a user forum, an online troubleshooter, and an easy utility for submitting support requests. Sounds good, right?

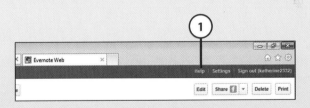

1. Log in if necessary and click Help in the top-right corner of the Evernote window.

2. Review the most recent updates that show the status of the Evernote server.

3. Click Knowledge Base to display a comprehensive listing of articles on various Evernote features and supported devices.

4. Click User Forum to display the community discussion boards, where you can get product information, ask support questions, learn from other users, and get tips and suggestions from Evernote users all over the world.

5. Click Troubleshooter to get help with a particular feature or technology.

6. Click Documentation to download Evernote Users Guides for Windows and Mac.

7. Click Chat with Evernote to start a chat session with an Evernote representative so that you can ask your question or explain your problem in real time. Note, however, that Chat with Evernote is available only weekdays between 9:00 am and 5:00 pm Pacific Time.

Checking Server Status

If you find that you're having trouble with Evernote—for example, your login is working slowly, your notes don't seem to be updating, or the notebook on your PC or phone doesn't seem to be syncing with the web—check the Evernote server status to see whether there's been a server problem or a maintenance period (in which the server may function slowly or be offline for a brief period of time). To display the Evernote server status, click Help on the Evernote home page.

Choose Your Troubleshooter

Evernote includes a number of troubleshooters you can use to get help solving problems in a number of key Evernote areas. For example, you can click Troubleshooter on the Help page and then select from various topics to choose what you want help using. For example, you can click Account Maintenance, Blackberry, iOS, Palm, Windows Phone, Mac, and other categories to display answers related to different features or technologies.

Submit a Support Request

If you're having trouble with Evernote and can't find the answers you need in the help system online, you can send a support request directly to the technical support staff at Evernote. If you are a Premium user, you may get a faster response than if you are a free user, but it's nice to know a real human being can help if you're feeling really stuck with a certain feature you want to use. Begin by displaying the Evernote Support window by clicking Help on the Evernote home page.

Submit a Ticket

To open a support inquiry, please identify your Evernote account.

E-mail [required]

Username

First [Given] Name

Last [Family] Name

SUBMIT   CANCEL

Inquiries from Premium Evernote accounts will receive a reply within one business day (Monday-Friday).

Sign up for a Premium subscription now.

Chat with Evernote

Evernote provides online chat support for users with Premium accounts, Monday through Friday between 9:00 am and 5:00 pm, US Pacific Time. Chat is currently only available in English.

1. Enter the email address you used to create your Evernote account.

2. Type your username.

3. Enter your first and last name.

4. Click Submit.

5. Click the Area arrow and choose the category that reflects what you're having a problem with.

6. Enter a brief summary of the problem.

7. Type the details of the problem, including what you were trying to do when the problem occurred, the computer or device you were using, and any error messages you received.

8. Click the link to attach a file—such as a screenshot or note.

9. Click Preview to preview the request.

10. Click Finish to submit the request. Evernote sends a confirmation email message to the email address you supplied, giving you a support ticket number as well as a copy of your submitted request.

Finding Your Answer

Evernote reviews the information you enter in the Summary and Details areas of the form and displays related information from the Knowledge Base. If you read through the information displayed and find the answer you need, click the I Found My Answer button displayed at the bottom of the information to cancel the request.

Downloading Evernote

After you create your Evernote account and learn the basics of using Evernote for the web, you'll want to download Evernote to your computer or mobile device so that you can take notes anywhere, anytime. Evernote offers a number of versions for free download:

- Windows

- Mac OS X

- iPhone and iPod touch

- iPad

- Android

- Android Tablet

- Windows Phone 7

- BlackBerry

- Blackberry PlayBook

- Pal Pre/Palm Pixi

The download process varies slightly, depending on whether you're downloading for a Windows PC, a Mac, or a mobile device.

Downloading Helpful Extras

You can also download additional Evernote utilities, such as Evernote Peek or the Evernote Web Clipper. Evernote Peek is a special app available for iPad 2 users who have a Smart Cover, enabling users to quiz themselves on information offered by various iPad 2 applications. The Web Clipper enables you to easily grab information from web pages that fascinate you and add them seamlessly to your Evernote notebook, complete with tags and the web address where you found the information. You learn more about the Web Clipper in Chapter 7, "Grabbing Web Clippings and Webcam Notes."

Downloading Evernote

When you're ready to download Evernote, begin by going to the Evernote home page. You'll find what you need right there.

1. Click the Get Evernote, It's Free button in the center of the window. Evernote automatically detects the web browser you are using and displays a download page for that browser.

2. Click Download Now. On a Windows PC, a message prompts you to choose whether you want to Run, Save, or Cancel the installation. On the Mac, you'll be asked to review the terms for using Evernote for Mac OS X and click Agree. After you do, Evernote begins downloading automatically.

3. On the PC, click Save. Evernote begins downloading to your computer.

Downloading and Installing Choices

If you prefer, you can download and install Evernote in one smooth process. Instead of clicking Save in the Windows download, for example, you can click Run. Or when you finish downloading the Mac version, you can drag Evernote to the Applications folder to install it seamlessly.

To make sure we're giving you the best coverage possible, we've decided to cover installation in Chapter 2, where you'll also learn about installing Evernote on your mobile devices (which require downloading from the appropriate marketplaces).

>> Go Further

CREATING A SPONSORED GROUP

If you work in a large organization—such as a school or large corporation— and you want all those you work with to be able to use Evernote, you can invest in a sponsored group to make setting up accounts for large numbers of users easy and affordable.

If you will have more than 25 users in your group, you can choose a Site Licensing option and pay annually, and Evernote offers a 50 percent discount to educational institutions and non-profit organizations. Costs range from $5 per month for one or two users in a sponsored account to $2.50 per user per month for groups of 100 or more. You can learn more about Evernote sponsored groups by going to www.evernote.com/about/sponsor.

Install Evernote easily
on your Mac...

...your Windows
Phone 7...

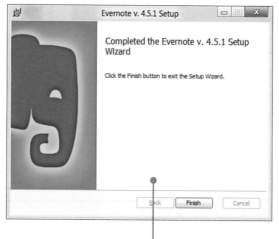

...your Windows PC, and more!

Evernote synchronizes the notes you add whether you're using a PC, the web, or phone so you always have access to the information you need. In this chapter, you get ready to roll with Evernote by completing the following tasks:

→ Evernote's Everywhere Approach
→ Installing Evernote on Your Windows or Mac computer
→ Installing Evernote on Your Mobile Phone
→ A Tour of the Evernote Window
→ Setting Evernote Options

Evernote Everywhere, on Everything!

The phenomenal success that Evernote is enjoying must have something to do with how easy it is to use just about anywhere you want to use it. Whether you have a PC, Mac, tablet PC, iPad, Android phone, Windows Phone 7, or Blackberry, you can easily download Evernote, capture and organize your notes, and sync everything back to the web so the most recent version of your notes are always available. Can you imagine having access to just what you need—budgets, proposals, holiday shopping lists, and more—wherever you need it?

Chapter 1, "Getting Started with Evernote," wrapped up with instructions on how to download Evernote to your computer. This chapter shows you how to install Evernote on just about anything you can imagine (except maybe your toaster). You'll also take a tour of the Evernote window on both a PC and Mac so that you can see the lay of the land.

Download and Install in One Fell Swoop

What exactly *is* a fell swoop? When you downloaded Evernote, you were given the option to Run or Save the program. If you clicked or tapped Save, a dialog box appeared so that you could save the program and install it later. If you clicked Run, Evernote downloaded and installed the program in one smooth process. If you have already installed Evernote, you can skip the next few sections (do not pass Go, do not collect $200) and take your tour of the Evernote window.

Evernote's Everywhere Approach

After you download and install Evernote on your various computers and devices, you may find yourself thinking in note form more often than you do right now. For example, grabbing a note from the web while you're working at your desktop PC, emailing a note to yourself from your phone when you have an item you want to remember, or even grabbing a snapshot of a diagram someone draws on a whiteboard and sending it to yourself from a remote site will be super easy.

No matter what kind of computer or device you're using, you can grab what you need—when it occurs to you—and send it to Evernote. Every so often (depending on how you configure the schedule), Evernote automatically syncs all of your notebooks with your notebooks on the web so that you always have access to the latest information you post. You can also click Sync to manually update your notes immediately if you don't want to wait on Evernote's automatic process.

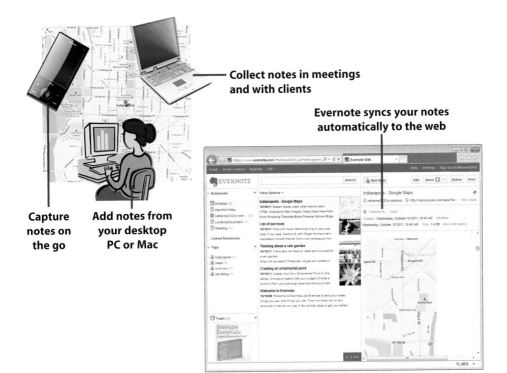

Collect notes in meetings and with clients

Evernote syncs your notes automatically to the web

Capture notes on the go

Add notes from your desktop PC or Mac

Installing Evernote on Your Windows or Mac Computer

The process of installing Evernote is different for PCs and Macs, but it involves only a few steps. In just a minute or two, you'll be able to create your first note! As you learned in Chapter 1, it's possible to download and install Evernote in one smooth step. If you have already installed Evernote, you can skip this section, but if you downloaded Evernote to your computer so that you could install it later, follow the instructions in this section to install the program on your computer.

Saving Evernote for Later

One of the great things about saving the Evernote installation utility to your computer instead of running it online is that you can make a copy of the Evernote installation file and store it on a flash drive so that you can easily install Evernote on other computers in your office or home—that way you always have access to the utility, whether you have access to the web or not.

Installing Evernote on a Windows PC

When you downloaded Evernote to your computer, the program was automatically saved to your Windows Downloads folder. You can now install Evernote by launching the installation utility and following the prompts on the screen.

1. Click Start in the lower-left corner of the Windows desktop.

2. Click Windows Explorer. (Alternatively, click the Windows Explorer icon in the Taskbar.)

3. Click the Downloads folder.

4. Scroll to display the Evernote program.

5. Double-click Evernote to launch the installation. The Open File dialog box appears.

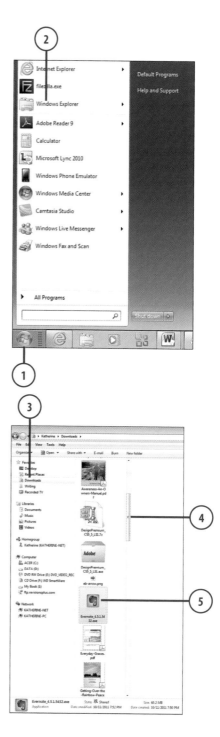

6. Click Run. If prompted, click Yes to give the installation utility permission to make changes to your computer. The utility extracts the Evernote files and then displays the Evernote Setup dialog box.

7. Review the user agreement.

8. Click the checkbox for I Accept the Terms in the License Agreement.

9. Click Install. The installation utility displays the progress of the installation.

10. Click Finish. The Evernote window opens, displaying your first note, which offers a number of tasks you may want to try right off the bat with Evernote.

Let's *Go*!

You might be tempted to dive right in and begin experimenting with Evernote. If so, great! Go ahead and we'll catch up in a minute. The next sections introduce installing Evernote on your Mac, tablet, and mobile device, and then this chapter wraps up with a tour of the Evernote windows.

Installing Evernote on a Mac

The process of downloading and installing Evernote on a Mac is seamless. Evernote prompts you to drag the Evernote icon to your Applications folder as soon as you download the installation file. Here are the steps.

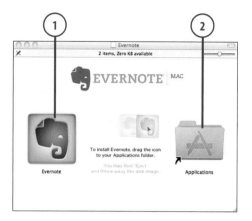

1. Click and drag the Evernote icon to the right.

2. Release the Evernote icon when it is on top of the Applications folder icon. The program begins installing automatically.

3. Click the Applications folder. Depending on the operating system you're running on your Mac, your image may look slightly different from the one shown here.

4. Click the Evernote icon.

5. A security warning tells you that the Evernote app was downloaded from the Internet and asks whether you want to open it. Click Open.

6. Evernote asks whether you want to install the Web Clipper so that you can easily clip notes from the web. Click Install Now. The utility installs and you'll be good to go, collecting web content for your Evernote notebooks.

Gray Evernote

The Evernote icon in the Applications folder first appears grayed out, as if it's not selectable, but what this actually means is that you haven't yet run the app for the first time. (Plus your Mac wants to make sure it's from a trusted source.) After you launch Evernote one time, you'll see the familiar Evernote green when you go to select the icon in the Applications folder.

ADDING THE WEB CLIPPER

>> Go Further

Earlier I mentioned the Web Clipper, an add-on utility (for both PCs and Macs) that you can use to clip content from web pages you visit and paste it quickly (with tags and web address) into your Evernote notes. When you install Evernote on a Mac that is running the Safari web browser, the Web Clipper installs automatically with the program. If you're running Firefox or Google Chrome on your Mac, however, you'll need to download the Web Clipper separately. (You learn more about how to use the Web Clipper in Chapter 7, "Grabbing Web Clippings and Webcam Notes.")

To find those clippers, go to the Evernote home page (www.evernote.com) and click Downloads in the upper-right corner of the window. Click Web Clipper. Scroll down to the bottom of the page and click the links to install the Evernote Google Chrome Extension or the Evernote Firefox Add-on.

Installing Evernote on Your Mobile Phone

The good news is that Evernote works on your smartphone, no matter what kind of smartphone you have, if you have the ability to surf the web. Although Evernote offers specific downloadable versions of the program for select smartphones—such as the iPhone, Android, Blackberry, and Windows Phone 7—any phone with web access can display Evernote on the web. This means you can capture great ideas no matter where you roam.

Installing Evernote on a Windows Phone 7

Although you can get to Evernote-for-Windows-Phone-7 info on the Evernote site, to download the app, you need to go to the Windows Phone 7 Marketplace. The best place to do this, of course, is through your phone.

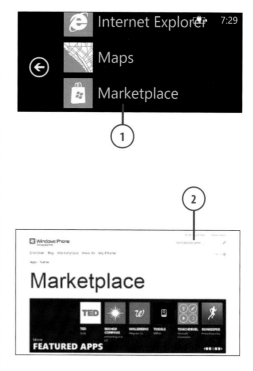

1. On your start screen of your phone, tap Marketplace. (If Marketplace doesn't appear on your start screen, swipe to the left to display the Apps, and then tap Marketplace in the alphabetical list.)

2. Tap the Search tool.

3. Type Evernote.

4. Tap Enter.

5. Tap Evernote.

6. Tap Get Free App. If you're using the web app, you'll be prompted to log in with your Windows Live ID and password and tap Sign In.

7. Choose whether you want to download the app directly to your phone (shown) or receive a link via email that you can use to install the program. The easiest method is to download the app to your phone, but if there's a reason you want to install the utility later, choose the email option.

8. Tap Next.

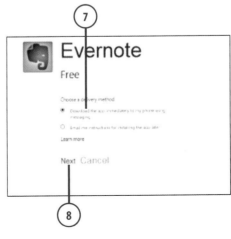

9. Choose the country where you are located.

10. Make sure your phone number is accurate.

11. Click the checkbox to authorize Evernote to download the app to your phone.

12. Click Next. The app installs and you are returned to the app page, where you can rate the app, tweet it, or post a link on your Facebook page about it.

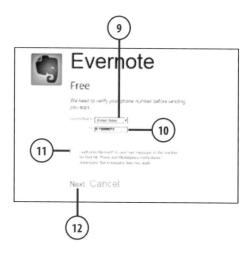

DOWNLOADS, DOWNLOADS EVERYWHERE

You actually have three different ways to download Evernote to your Windows Phone 7:

- On your Windows Phone 7, you can tap Marketplace, tap Search, enter Evernote in the Marketplace Search box, and tap Install;

- On your Windows Phone 7 or in your web browser, you can go to the Windows Phone Marketplace online (www.windowsphone.com) and search for Evernote and download it (that's the process shown in this section);

- Or you can launch the Zune software on your PC and access the marketplace—and find and download Evernote—through that program.

>>> Go Further

Installing Evernote on the iPhone and iPod Touch

The Evernote downloads page does include a link directly to the iTunes App Store so that you can install Evernote seamlessly on your Apple device without wandering all over the web. The only requirement is that you first have iPhone OS 3.1.2 or later installed on your phone.

Some of the benefits of Evernote for the iPhone, iPod Touch, and iPad 2 include the ability to flick, tap, and pinch your way through notebook and note display; display notes in landscape or portrait mode; create and save searches; work with notebook stacks and tags; record up to 90 minutes of audio notes; and much more.

1. On your iPhone or iPod Touch, go to the iPhone App Store and tap the Search icon at the bottom of the screen.

2. Tap in the Search field.

3. Type Evernote.

4. When you locate the Evernote app icon in the search field results, tap it.

5. Tap Install.

6. Log in to your Apple ID account by typing your password.

7. Tap OK. The Evernote app installation icon appears in your applications list, ready to launch.

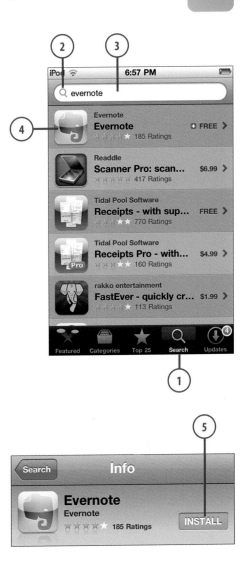

Installing on Android

Installing Evernote on your Android phone gives you note-taking and notebook organizing ability on the go, anywhere you need it. You'll need Android OS 1.6 to take advantage of Evernote in its latest incarnation. To install Evernote on your Android phone, go to the Android Marketplace, search for Evernote, and tap to download and install the free app.

>>> Go Further

ADDING EVERNOTE TO YOUR TABLET

You can also add Evernote easily to your tablet so you have a large, touch-driven screen space where you can drag and drop your notes from notebook to notebook. Separate versions of Evernote are available for Android Tablets (OS 1.6 and later) and for BlackBerry PlayBooks (Tablet OS).

To install Evernote for your particular tablet, go to the Evernote home page (www.evernote.com) and tap Downloads in the upper-right corner of the window. In the For Mobile Devices list on the left side of the screen, tap the version you need (Android Tablet or BlackBerry PlayBook). On the next page that appears, tap the link that takes you directly to your tablet's market-place, where you can download the free Evernote app.

In addition to the Evernote versions I have installed on my desktop PC, my Windows Phone 7.5, and my MacBook Pro, I'm running Evernote on my Dell Inspiron Duo tablet that is currently running Windows 8 Developer Preview, and it runs like a charm. (Note, however, that Windows 8 is pre-beta software, so we're not using it in the examples in this book.) To install Evernote on the Windows tablet, I simply went to the Evernote home page and downloaded the Windows version of the software.

A Tour of the Evernote Window

As you can imagine, Evernote looks somewhat different on the various devices and computers it supports, but the basic functionality of the program is similar among the different formats. In this section you get a quick look at Evernote on the different hardware platforms. This will give you a sense of what to find and where, before you dive in and begin capturing your great ideas.

Evernote on the PC

Evernote for Windows displays all the tools you need within easy reach of your mouse, displaying your notebooks in a panel on the left side of the screen; individual notes in the column in the center; and the selected note in the panel on the right. Tools stretch above the top of the notes area, and menus contain the options you need for working with the notes and notebooks you create.

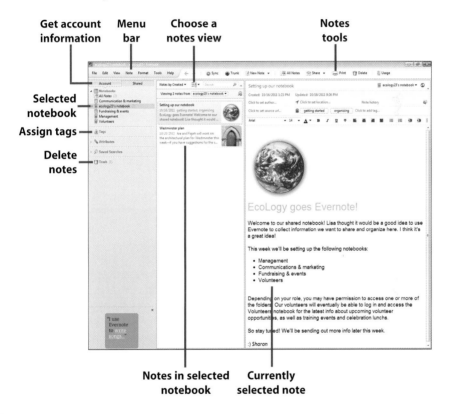

Get account information
Menu bar
Choose a notes view
Notes tools

Selected notebook

Assign tags

Delete notes

Notes in selected notebook
Currently selected note

Evernote on Mac OS X

Evernote for the Mac offers all your tools in a streamlined, easy-to-use Mac interface. The tools at the top of the window are designed to give you the information you need quickly. A usage status tool shows you at a glance your current monthly usage; you can easily switch among views or share your notes and notebooks. The basic layout of the screen—notebooks on the left, notes in the center, and the selected note on the right—is identical to the layout you find in the Windows version.

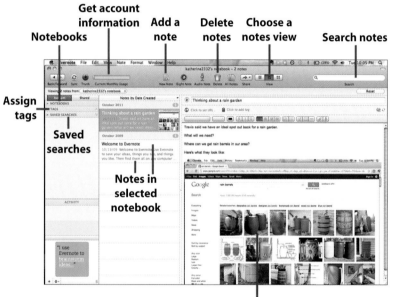

Evernote on Mobile Devices

Evernote for your phone is optimized to make the most of the small screen display on mobile devices. You can still review notes, create new notes, organize your notebooks, and much more.

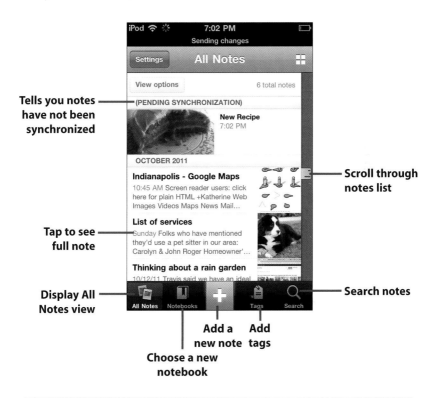

Tells you notes have not been synchronized

Scroll through notes list

Tap to see full note

Display All Notes view

Search notes

Add a new note

Add tags

Choose a new notebook

Viewing Notes on Your Mobile Phone

If you're using the free version of Evernote on your phone, when you open one of your notebooks, you'll see a listing of note titles, but to retrieve the entire note, Evernote needs access to the web. Whenever you are connected to the web, however, Evernote takes care of synchronizing your notes automatically.

Evernote on Non-Smart Phones

Even if your phone isn't a smartphone, if it has web capability, you can use it to work with your Evernote notebooks. Go to http://evernote.com/m to find out more.

Setting Evernote Options

Now that you've installed Evernote and had a look around the Evernote window, you can change some of the program options so it will work the way you want it to while you're adding and organizing your notes. Evernote options are straightforward, and you'll find them in the Tools menu in the Windows version of Evernote (these options aren't available for the Mac version).

Customizing Evernote Startup

After you download and install Evernote, you can tweak some of the startup settings so that the program launches when you want it to and checks for updates on a regular basis.

1. Click Tools.

2. Click Options.

3. In the General tab, click the first option if you want to launch Evernote when you start your computer.

4. Click the option to update automatically to the next pre-release version of Evernote when it is available. Pre-release means that the Evernote version will be part of a beta program in which users like you test the software to help Evernote find and fix any bugs before the program is in wide release. If you'd rather wait for the next release version of Evernote, leave this option unchecked.

5. Click the option to check for program updates.

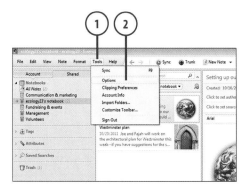

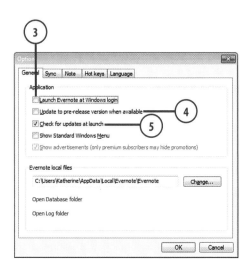

6. Click the option to display Evernote in a Windows XP screen layout. Selecting this option changes the menu bar and Evernote tools row to a Windows XP-like display; the rounded tabs and gradient colors are removed and you'll see Windows XP's clean lines instead.

7. Click the Change button to choose a different folder for Evernote to store notes on your computer. Note that even if you change the Local Files location, Evernote still stores your notes in the cloud if you have created a synchronized notebook. If you choose to create a local notebook (which means your notes are stored only on the computer you used to create the notebook), your files will be stored in the Local Files folder. (For more about creating synchronized and local notebooks, see Chapter 9, "Creating and Managing Notebooks.")

8. Click OK.

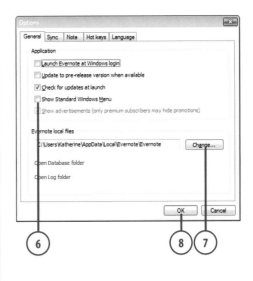

Seeing What You've Been Doing with Evernote

If you want to read through a log of actions you've taken in Evernote (perhaps you want to remember whether you added an item yesterday to this notebook, or you want to get a sense of the last time another user logged in), you can take a look at the Evernote log file. Click Tools and click Options, and in the General tab, click Open Log folder. Review the files as needed to find what you need and then click the close box to return to Evernote.

Setting Sync Options

As mentioned earlier, one of the great features of Evernote is the way in which everything is synchronized for you so that you always have access to the most recent information you've captured—on any device. You can change the Sync options if you like to change when Evernote synchronizes your notes and how the operation happens. With the Options dialog box open on the screen (click Tools, Options), follow these steps:

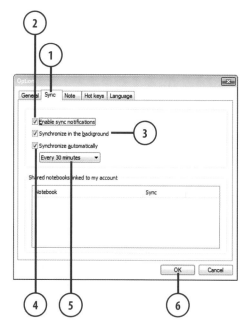

1. Click the Sync tab.

2. Click the option to have Evernote notify you when your notebooks are synchronized with the web.

3. Click the option to enable Evernote to synchronize in the background while you're working on other things.

4. Click the option to have Evernote sync your notes automatically.

5. Set how often Evernote synchronizes your files. Every 30 minutes is the default value, but you can also choose Every 15 minutes, Every hour, and Every day.

6. Click OK.

Synchronizing Manually

You can also synchronize your notes manually; for example, when you've added a note you want to share with other notebooks right away. You can synchronize your notes by pressing F9 or by clicking the Sync tool in the Evernote toolbar. It's not a bad idea to click Sync right before you close Evernote, just to make sure that your most recent notes are synced to the web.

>> Go Further

HOW EVERNOTE SYNCHRONIZES THE NOTES YOU CREATE

Evernote makes keeping your notebooks up-to-date easy no matter where you grab the notes and in which notebook you put them. When you create a new notebook in Evernote, the notebook by default is a synchronized notebook, which means that any notes you add are synced automatically with your Evernote notebooks on the Evernote servers out on the web. Your other computers and devices—such as your PC, your tablet, and your phone—will receive the updates and be synchronized to the web notebooks automatically when they are connected to the Internet.

If you add notes to Evernote when you're not connected to the web, the notes won't be synchronized to your notebooks on the web until you connect to the Internet again.

You can synchronize notes manually, though, if you've just added something that you want to make sure is made available in all your notebooks.

Saying Goodbye to Evernote

On the off chance that you want to do away with your Evernote account (or perhaps you've created more than one and you want to remove the one you no longer need), you can deactivate your account by going to the Evernote home page (www.evernote.com), logging in with your username and password, and clicking Settings. Click the Deactivate Account link and then confirm the process on the next page. The good news is that you can reactivate a deactivated account if you want; just log in using the same email address and password you used previously, and follow the steps Evernote offers you.

It's Not All Good

The bad news about this process for privacy advocates is that Evernote says it doesn't delete your notes. Fortunately, you still have options. If you're concerned about information you've saved to your notebooks still being out there in the Internet ether, you can always reactivate your account, delete the notes you're worried about, and deactivate Evernote once again.

Click New Note on your
Windows or Mac computer

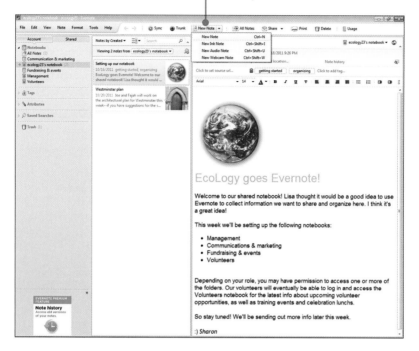

Assign note attributes
in the note header

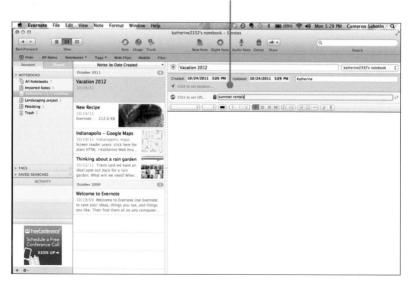

Adding a note is a simple task in Evernote—
by typing, pasting, emailing, and tweeting—
and you can tag your notes to categorize
them and find them easily later. In this chapter, you learn to create and tag your first
notes by completing the following tasks:

→ Creating a New Note

→ Typing or Pasting Note Content

→ Adding, Assigning, and Removing Tags

→ Emailing Notes to Yourself

→ Tweeting Your Notes

Capturing and Tagging Your First Notes

Now that you have installed Evernote and learned the ins and
outs of using it on your own system—whichever computer or
device that might be—you are ready to begin taking notes!
Capturing a note in Evernote is a super flexible process. You
can type a note, copy and paste a note, record yourself speaking out out loud, sketch or handwrite a note, or add photos to
notes. After you add the content you want to remember, you
can add tags to the note so that you can find the note again
easily later in a search.

Yes, but How Secure Is It?

All the notes and notebooks you create in Evernote are stored on Evernote-managed, secure servers Santa Clara, California. Your notes aren't publicly available—to other users or search engines—unless you create and publish a notebook as a public notebook. If you want to add a layer of security to your notes, you can select note text, right-click, and choose Encrypt Selected Text. After you enter a passphrase and click OK, Evernote encrypts the text and enables you to change it only if you first enter the passphrase you selected.

Creating a New Note

No matter which computer or device you're using, Evernote makes starting a new note as simple as possible. For the examples in this chapter, we'll use a Windows computer, but add in Mac and mobile tips along the way.

Different Notes, Different Chapters

In this chapter we start out showing you how to create a simple text note, but you can easily add other types of notes to Evernote, too. In Chapter 6, "Inking Your Notes," you'll learn how to write your notes and sketch them by hand—directly into your Evernote notebook. In Chapter 7, you'll find out about "Grabbing Web Clippings and Webcam Notes," and in Chapter 8, you'll learn about "Recording Audio Notes."

Starting a New Note

So what kind of notes do you want to capture? Maybe you've finally learned how to make apple butter and you want to save the recipe so you can try it next fall. Or you had an idea for a new project you want to start—and you want to save the materials list to your notebook. Or perhaps you are working with a group on a new version of your club newsletter, and you all will be contributing articles on the fly. Whatever your reason, adding a new note is a simple task in all versions of Evernote.

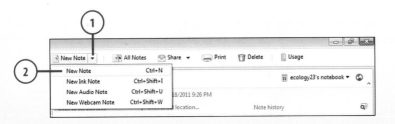

1. In the Evernote window, click the New Note arrow.

2. Click New Note. The new note window opens and the title area is selected so that you can start right off adding a title for your new note.

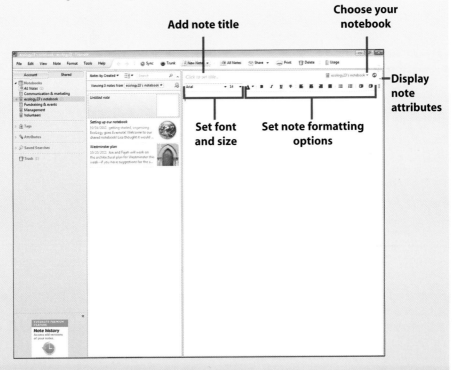

Add note title

Choose your notebook

Display note attributes

Set font and size

Set note formatting options

Phoning in Your Note

If you're using a smartphone, open a new note by tapping the New Note icon (+) in the tool area of the phone display.

What's the Limit?

Evernote does have a monthly limit to the number of notebooks, notes, and tags you create. Whether you have a free or premium Evernote account, you need to keep your creative vibe under 250 notebooks, 100,000 total notes, or 10,000 tags. That seems possible, right?

Adding a Note Title

Searching for the notes you need in Evernote is a simple process, so you may not think a title matters much. Although your tags and searches are likely to help you find what you need, naming your notes in such a way that the titles remind you of the content you're capturing is always a good idea. This is also helpful when you're sharing your notes and want others to be able to see quickly which notes are likely to have what they need.

1. In the New Note window, click in the Click to Set Title area. If you have typed text into the body of the note already, Evernote automatically uses that first segment of text as the note title.

2. Type the title for the note.

Where Do You Want to Store That?

If you have created multiple notebooks (you learn how to do this in Chapter 9, "Creating and Managing Notebooks"), you can choose the notebook in which you want to store the new note by clicking the arrow to the right of the notebook selection and clicking your choice. Evernote also makes it easy to move notes from notebook to notebook. (You also learn to do that in Chapter 9.)

Adding Author Name and Location

You can add what Evernote calls *attributes* to your notes to include additional information so that you know who created the note (which is particularly useful if you are working with shared notebooks) and where the note was created.

1. In the new note window, click the attributes arrow. This displays one row of note attributes.

2. Click the arrow a second time. Now you see all the note attributes for the new note.

3. Click in the Click to Set Author area and type the author name.

4. Click in the Click to Set Location area. The Enter a Default Location dialog box appears.

5. Click Enter a Default Location Now.

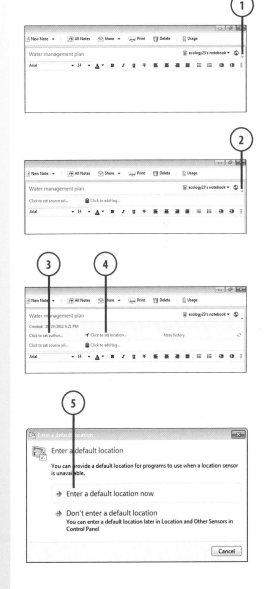

6. Type your ZIP code.

7. Choose your country or region.

8. If you want to enter your address, click the Address arrow and enter your address, city, and state.

9. Click Apply.

10. Click the Close box.

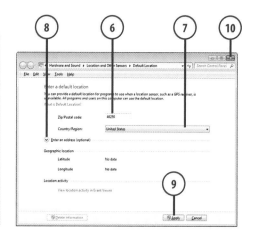

Going to the Source

Later you will learn to use web clipping to add notes from the web to your Evernote pages. One of the note attributes' displays gives you the option to set the source URL of the information you enter. Here you can paste the web address of the site you're clipping from, and it will always stay with the note saved in your Evernote notebook.

Adding Attributes the Mobile Way

When you are adding a note from your mobile device, you can choose the notebook to which you want to add the note and select the tags you want to assign, but you can't change the other note attributes like those available to you in your Windows or Mac versions.

Typing or Pasting Note Content

Now comes the fun part. What do you want to add to your Evernote page? Are you researching new hiking boots, grabbing content for a new album you're creating, planning a great dinner party, or planning a family vacation? Or maybe your notes will be about a project you're working on or new business opportunity you're considering.

Whatever your interest, the next step is to add the content to your Evernote page. You can do this by typing the note, copying and pasting content into the note, or simply dragging and dropping content to the waiting page.

How Big Can Your Notes Be?

Evernote does have a maximum size for individual notes, but it's a high limit. If you are a free account user, the largest note you can create is 25 MB, including any files you attach to the note. If you are a premium account user, you can create notes up to 50 MB in size.

SAVING AND SYNCING YOUR NOTES

When you're finished adding content to a note, there's no need to save the note; Evernote does it automatically for you. You can simply click the note by clicking the close box or click a different note you want to view. Evernote automatically saves the note and syncs it with the Evernote server so that all your notebook versions have the same content.

You can control how often Evernote syncs your notebooks by clicking Tools, choosing Options, and clicking the Sync tab. Make sure the Synchronize Automatically checkbox is selected, and click the arrow and choose how often you want Evernote to synchronize your notebooks—from every 15 minutes to once a day. Click OK to save your changes and return to your notes.

Typing Note Content

There's not too much that's easier than adding a note in Evernote. Just click in the note area and start typing. Let's try it out.

1. Click in the note window.
2. Type the text you want to add.

Adding Images

You can also add images from your desktop by dragging them and dropping them into your Evernote note. You'll learn more about working with images in Chapter 5, "Adding and Working with Images."

>> Go Further

GRABBING ISIGHT NOTES ON YOUR MAC

On the Mac, you can add an iSight note that adds a photo (taken by the webcam) directly to the Evernote notebook you choose. Click iSight Note at the top of the Evernote window, and the Snapshot window opens. Click Take Photo Snapshot in the lower-left corner of the window, and a red bar appears, counting down 3, 2, 1, and then the snapshot is taken. The image appears in the Snapshot window, and if you want to keep it, then click Add to Evernote. If you want to delete the image instead of adding it, click Discard.

If you keep the iSight Note, it is added to a new note in Evernote. Add the title and any other note attributes, such as author, tags, or text, and close the note. Evernote will automatically sync the note with the server and your notebooks on other computers and devices.

Dragging and Dropping Note Content

Another great—and super easy—feature of Evernote enables you to drag and drop content to your Evernote note. You might do this, for example, when you're working with a file open on the screen and you want to make a mental note to remember something you've just read. You can just highlight the idea and drag it right to your notebook. Sweet.

1. Create a new note in Evernote.

2. Add a note title if you want.

3. Highlight the content you want to copy to Evernote. Whether you're using a PC or Mac, press and hold Shift and drag the highlighted content to the new note page.

4. Release the mouse button on the Evernote note page.

Notes and Notebooks: Happily Ever After

One of the great things about Evernote is that it doesn't force you into organizing your notes in any particular way. If you simply want to create hundreds of notes and use Evernote's search capability to find what you need, you don't really need to create notebooks. However, most people (and I'm one) like to create notebooks to store notes that are related to specific topics. You might have one notebook for a work project, for example, and have another notebook to store information related to your kids' sports activities. In Chapter 9, "Creating and Managing Notebooks," you learn how to create, organize, import, and stack your notebooks so that you can easily find the notes you need.

Adding Note Links

As you continue adding notes, you may notice a pattern developing. Perhaps you want to link the notes so that you can access them sequentially, one after another. You can easily add a link to a note by following these steps.

1. Select the note for which you want to create a link.

2. Right-click the note.

3. Click Copy Note Link.

4. Click the note where you want to paste the link.

5. Right-click the note area.

6. Click Paste. Evernote adds the note name and link to the note window.

Copying a Note Link on a Mac

 If you want to copy the note link on your Mac version of Evernote, press Control while you click the note in the Evernote window. In the list that appears, click Copy Note Link.

Create a Note Index

You can do lots of things with note links to make your life easier. For example, you can create a new note that includes a collection of links all related to a specific topic; that way you can always find the notes you need easily.

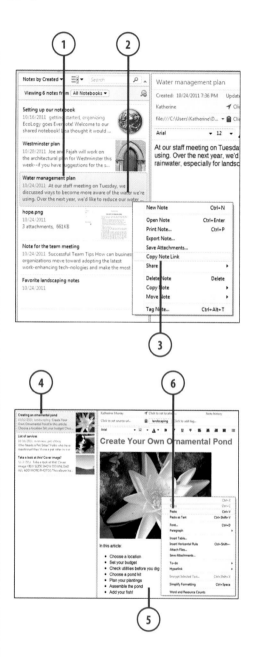

It's Not All Good

Linking Your Notes for Others, Too

When you use Copy Note Link, a link to that note is placed in memory, and you can paste it wherever you want. Keep in mind that the note links are just for notes within your account, however; they aren't for sharing with other users. If you send friends or teammates the link you copied, they won't be able to get to the note content in your notebook. You can create a shared link and send it to other users by right-clicking the note and choosing Copy Shared Note URL To Clipboard in the Sharing menu. Now you can paste *that* link into the message you share with others and they will be able to view the note content you posted. If you've opted to share the notebook publicly, users won't need an Evernote account to see your notes; if you have decided to share a private notebook, other users will need to log in with their Evernote accounts before they can view the information you've shared.

Adding, Assigning, and Removing Tags

Tags give you an easy way to categorize your notes so that you can find them again later. When you add a tag to a note, you assign a small word or phrase that then becomes available for other notes. You can click and type a tag to add it to a note, or you can drag and drop a tag from the tag list to the note to tag it. You can also easily rename and delete tags as needed.

Tagging Your Note

Earlier in this chapter you learned about note attributes, those bits of information such as the author name or location you can add to a note you create. You can easily add tags to your note by clicking and typing the tags you want to add in the note attributes area.

1. Click the note you want to tag.
2. In the note attributes, click the Click to Add Tag link.

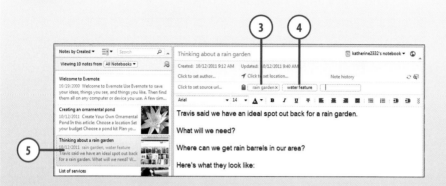

3. Type the tag you want to add and press Enter.

4. Type another tag if you like and press Enter.

5. Evernote records the tags and displays them in the note summary in the center of the Evernote window.

Adding and Assigning New Tags

If you have a specific set of tags you want to apply to the content you add in your notebooks, you can create tags directly and then apply them to the notes you add. Evernote lists the tags you create in the Tags area in the left panel of the Evernote window.

1. Click Tags to display the list of existing tags.

2. Right-click the Tags area.

3. Click Create Tag. The Create Tag dialog box appears.

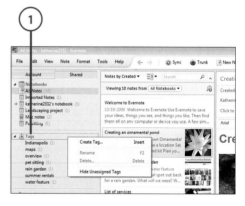

4. Type a name for the new tag.

5. Click OK. Evernote adds the tag to the list in the left panel.

6. Assign the new tag to your notes by dragging the tag to the note and releasing the mouse button.

Renaming Tags

You can easily rename tags you create in Evernote. Simply right-click the tag and choose Rename Tag from the list that appears. Note that when you change a tag, however, the tag is changed on all your notes. For example, if you change the tag *water feature* to *waterscape*, all notes that previously had the *water feature* tag will now have the tag *waterscape* applied to the note content.

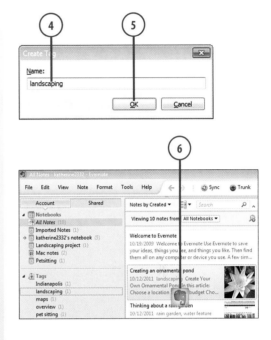

Removing and Deleting Tags

The possibility exists that you will assign tags to notes and then think better of your choice. Luckily you can easily remove tags you've assigned by mistake. You may also want to delete tags you no longer need. Both procedures are simple.

1. Click the note that includes the tag you want to remove.

2. In the note attributes, select the tag you want to delete.

3. Click the X to the right of the tag name. Evernote removes the tag from the note.

4. When you want to delete a tag completely so that it is removed from all notes that include it, right-click it in the Tags area of the left panel.

5. Click Delete. The Confirm Action dialog box appears, letting you know that continuing this action will remove the tag and all sub-tags associated with it. Click Delete Tag to remove the tag, and it disappears from the Tags list on the left side of the Evernote window.

>>> Go Further

ASSIGNING MULTIPLE TAGS AT ONCE

You can also use a tool in the Note menu to assign multiple tags at once. Begin by selecting the note you want to tag, and then click Note to display the Note menu. Click Tag, and the Assign Tags dialog box appears.

Go through the list of tags in the dialog box and click the checkboxes of any you want to assign to the selected note. You can also click Select All if you want to assign all tags at once.

If you want to add a new tag, click in the Add a New Tag box and type the tag you want to add. Click Add to add it to the list. When you're finished, click OK, and Evernote adds all the tags to the note you selected.

Emailing Notes to Yourself

When you are out and about in the world—armed with your mobile phone or your tablet or netbook— you'll likely find all kind of items you want to add to your Evernote notebooks. Maybe you're at a meeting and you want to grab a photo of a logo on your cell phone and send it directly to your Evernote account. Or perhaps a client sends you an email message you want to be sure to include in a notebook about a project you're working on. In both of those situations—and many, many more—you can email your notes directly to your Evernote notebook, using a unique email address Evernote provides for you.

Limits to Your Note Mailing

Evernote does have a limit to the number of emails you can send to your Evernote address per day. If you have a free Evernote account, you can send up to 50 emails a date to your Evernote notebooks; if you are a premium account user, you can sent up to 250 emails per day. The totals reset at midnight, Pacific time, each day.

Finding Your Evernote Email Address on the Web

Evernote automatically assigns a unique email address to your Evernote account. To find the email address, log in to Evernote on the web and go to your account Settings.

1. Go to the Evernote home page (www.evernote.com) and click Sign In.

2. Click Settings.

3. In the Emailing to Evernote section, the email address will be displayed. Click the link to open a new email message window, add text in the Subject line, and click Send to test the account.

Reset Your Email Address

If you aren't thrilled, for whatever reason, with the email address Evernote has assigned to your notebook—or if you're worried that you may have inadvertently shared the email address with others—you can have Evernote reset your email address. Log in to Evernote on the web and click Settings; then click the Reset Incoming Email button in the Account Summary page.

TABLE 3.1   FIND YOUR EMAIL ADDRESS IN DESKTOP OR MOBILE APPS

On Your	Do the Following
Android	Tap the Evernote menu and Settings
iPad	Tap Settings, scroll down and tap the Evernote email address
iPhone	Tap All Notes in the Evernote app menu, and tap Settings
Mac	In the Evernote app menu, tap Account Info tab
Windows	Click Tools and click Account Info

Sending Notes to Yourself by Email

After you find your email address, be sure to add it to your phone, your email client, and all your web accounts and mobile devices. That way you'll be ready to email your notes when inspiration strikes.

1. On your phone or desktop mail client, open a new email message.

2. In the To box, enter or select your Evernote email address.

3. Add the note content to the body of the message.

4. Click or tap Send. The note is added to your default notebook in Evernote and will be synced with your notebook on all computers and devices you use.

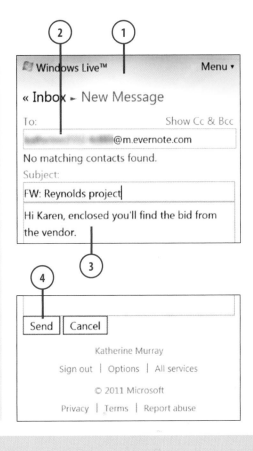

>>> Go Further

FILE AND TAG YOUR EMAILED NOTES AUTOMATICALLY

You can tell Evernote which notebook you want to save a specific note to by adding an @ sign and the name of the notebook to the subject of your email message. For example, to add an article about creating a rain garden to your Landscaping notebook, you could use the following subject line:

Create a Rain Garden @Landscaping

If you want to automatically tag the note you are emailing to your Evernote notebook, you can do so by adding hashtags to the message subject line. If you want to add the tags *water feature* and *garden design* to the note you're emailing to yourself, your subject line could look like this:

Create a Rain Garden @Landscaping #water feature #garden design

Note that any tags you use as part of an email message must already exist in Evernote.

Tweeting Your Notes

If you're a Twitter fan, you are already aware of the waves and waves (and waves!) of information available in those short, 140-character tweets. Whether your interest is technology, turtles, or truffles, you will find a constant stream of information tweeting your way. When you find tweets that you want to save to your Evernote notebook, you can retweet the post or send it as a private direct message directly to your Evernote account.

Setting Up Your Twitter Stream

The first step involves signing up to follow Evernote on Twitter. Then the Evernote account will follow you back, and you'll be ready to begin! Here are the steps:

1. Go to Twitter at www.twitter.com.

2. Search for myEN.

3. Click Follow. Almost instantly, Evernote will Follow you and send you a direct message.

4. Click Messages.

5. Click the link in the Evernote message to set up your Evernote account to receive tweets.

6. Click Link Accounts.

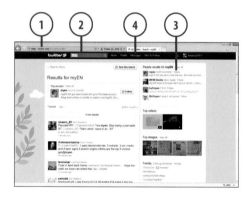

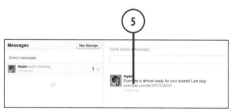

Checking Twitter Info

After you click Link Accounts, your Evernote Settings are displayed. To review the information from Twitter, click the Twitter category in the left side of the window. If you want to unlink Twitter from your Evernote account at a later time, click Remove Twitter Account.

Tweeting to Evernote

After your account is set up and ready to go, you can just tweet your information directly into your default Evernote notebook. You can send Twitter messages two different ways: You can send a public tweet and send it to your Evernote notebook at the same time, or you can send a private direct message directly to your Evernote notebook (for your eyes only).

1. In your Twitter account, click in the update box.

2. Type the information you want to tweet publicly.

3. Add @myEN to the end of your tweet.

4. Click Tweet. The tweet is added automatically to your default Evernote notebook.

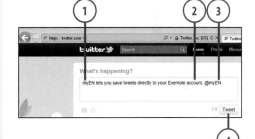

Sending Direct Messages to Evernote

If you don't want to share your tweets with the world but you want to add them to your Evernote notebook, you can send yourself a direct message from Twitter.

1. In Twitter, click Messages.

2. Click the New Message button.

3. In the Message window, address the message to myEN.

4. Enter your note in the text box.

5. Click Send.

TEXTING TO EVERNOTE

You can also use the SMS capability on your phone to send text messages directly to your Evernote account. Create a new text message and address the message to 40404.

Now in the body of the text message, type **d myEN**, followed by the note you want to send. Tap Send, and the next time your notebook synchronizes, you'll see your text messages in your default Evernote notebook!

This technique does, of course, require a Twitter account. If you want to text notes from your phone to your Evernote account without using Twitter, you can send text messages to the email address Evernote assigns to your account.

>>> Go Further

Easily assign new colors
and formats to your notes

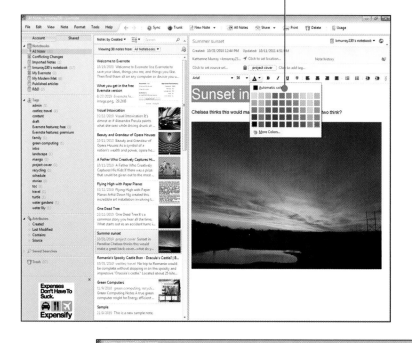

Choose the
look you
want for
your note
text

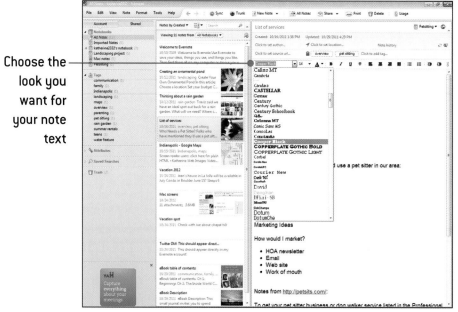

With a few simple clicks, you can edit your notes and apply formatting features to make them really stand out. In this chapter, you learn how to edit and format note content by completing the following tasks:

Editing and Formatting Notes

Maybe you aren't too worried about getting all the Ps and Qs right in your notes if you are just using them to collect information you may use sometime down the road. But if you're working on a project, sharing notes with others, or collaborating on a research assignment where the accuracy and the format of your notes matter, you'll appreciate the tools Evernote provides for editing and enhancing the content you collect.

This chapter focuses on the various tools and techniques you'll use when you want to change or correct your information or create a new look for your note text.

Editing the Content of a Note

If you've ever used a word processing program (and I'm guessing you have) the editing tools in Evernote will be no surprise to you. You can click and insert new information, remove items you don't need, copy and paste note content, and check the spelling of what you've added. It's a breeze.

Correcting Note Text

The easiest editing changes happen when you just click and type—as in, click in the paragraph, press Backspace to delete that extra S, and you're done.

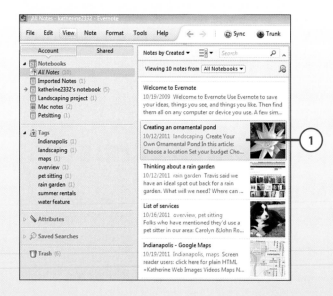

1. Double-click the note you want to change. The note opens in its own window.

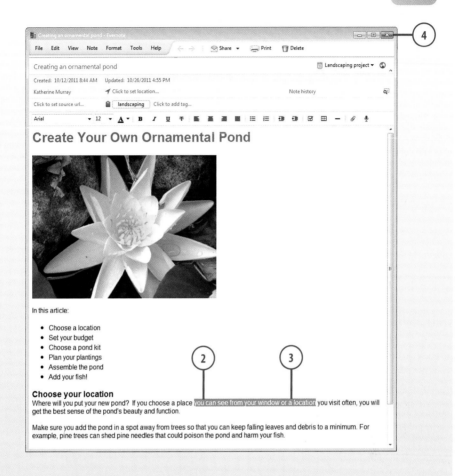

2. Click to position the cursor where you want to make the change or highlight the text you want to work with.

3. Make the changes you want to make by pressing Delete or typing new text.

4. Click the close button to close the note.

Opening a Note

You can make editing changes in a note whether you edit the note in the right panel of notes view or you double-click and edit the note in its own window. If the note has a lot of content, however, you may find it easier to locate and change note text when you open the note and edit it in the note window.

EVERNOTE EDITING SHORTCUT KEYS

Task	Windows	Mac	Description
Undo	Ctrl+Z	⌘+Z	Reverses last editing operation
Redo	Ctrl+Y	⌘+Shift+Z	Repeats last editing operation
Select All	Ctrl+A	⌘+A	Selects all content in the current note
Cut	Ctrl+X	⌘+X	Removes selected content and places it on the clipboard
Copy	Ctrl+C	⌘+C	Makes a copy of the selected content and places the copy on the clipboard
Paste	Ctrl+V	⌘+V	Pastes the content on the clipboard at the cursor location

Moving and Removing Note Content

You can easily move note content from place to place, and you have a couple of choices for the way in which you do that. You might select text and drag it to a new location, or you could select a paragraph, cut the text—which places it on the clipboard—and then paste the content somewhere else on the note page.

1. Open the note you want to work with.

2. Select the content you want to move.

3. Drag and drop the content to the new location.

4. If you need to paste the content at a point later in the note, you can copy or cut and paste the information using the Edit menu tools. Select the text and click Edit.

5. Click Copy to place a copy of the selected content on the clip-board.

6. Move to the new note location and click to position the cursor.

7. Click Edit.

8. Click Paste to paste the content in the new location.

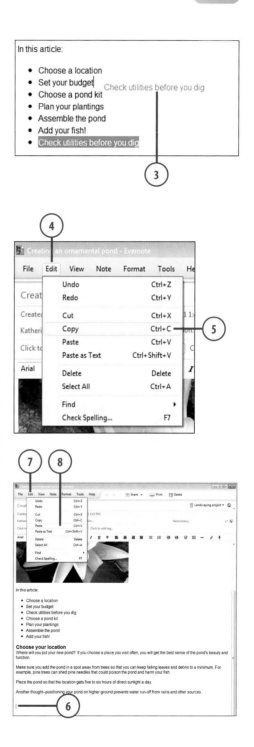

Checking the Spelling of Your Note

Evernote also includes a spelling checker so that you can make sure the spelling of your note content is as accurate as possible. The Spelling Checker is simple but functional; Evernote scans your note quickly and alerts you if anything is misspelled, and suggests spelling alternatives. You can add new words to the dictionary as you go, if you have unique spellings that you will use again and again.

1. Open the note you want to spell check.

2. Click Edit to open the Edit menu.

3. Click Check Spelling. The Spell Check dialog box appears if Evernote finds a spelling problem.

4. Click a word to choose a different spelling.

5. Click in the box to type a new spelling.

6. Click Add to Dictionary to add the word as spelled to your Evernote dictionary.

7. Click Ignore Once to ignore the spelling at this occurrence in the note.

8. Click Ignore All to ignore this spelling everywhere in the current note.

9. Click Change to change the spelling of the word to the spelling listed in the Suggestions box for this occurrence.

10. Click Change All to change all occurrences of the spelling in this note. Repeat these steps as prompted for each misspelling in the note.

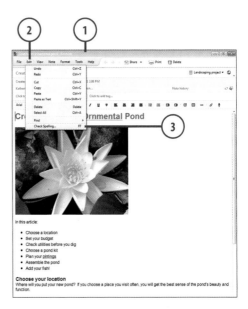

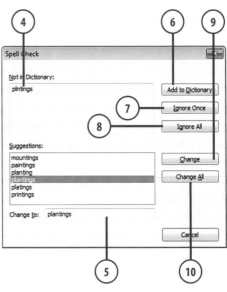

11. When all the misspellings are corrected, Evernote lets you know. Click OK to complete the spelling checker.

Inserting Date and Time

For some notes you create, having a date and time stamp can be helpful. This enables you to see which notes you've added most recently and perhaps help you decide between two notes. If you're using Evernote on a Windows PC, you can add the data and time automatically to your note by pressing the Ctrl+; shortcut key.

Finding and Replacing Note Text

Evernote has a wonderful search capability that extends beyond the current note and reaches through all your notebooks to help you find just what you need. In this section we'll take a look at how Evernote makes it easy to find what you're looking for in the current note.

Searching Notebooks

Chapter 10, "Finding and Viewing Notes Your Way," shows you how to search by different characteristics so that you can find the content you're looking for among your various notebooks. You'll also learn to save your searches so that you can use the same search criteria again in the future.

Finding Note Text

When you need to find a specific product name or phrase in the current note, you enter the word or phrase in a Find box and Evernote highlights the search results you're looking for. You can easily move through the different results and find the instance you want by using the tools that appear at the bottom of the note window.

1. Select the note you want to use.

2. Click the Edit menu.

3. Point to Find and Replace.

4. Click Find Within Note.

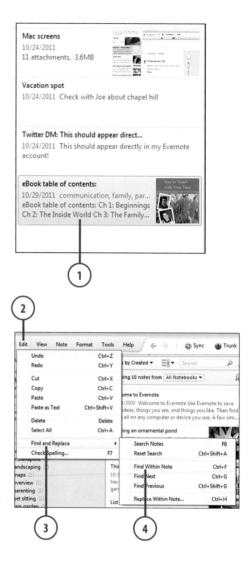

5. Type the word or phrase you're looking for.

6. Click Next to move to the next occurrence in the text.

Finding Note Content Quickly

 You can use shortcut keys on both Windows PCs and Macs 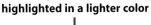 when you want to locate note text quickly. On the PC, press Ctrl+F to open the find text box; on the Mac, press ⌘+F.

Evernote highlights the first occurrence in a dark color

Subsequent matches are highlighted in a lighter color

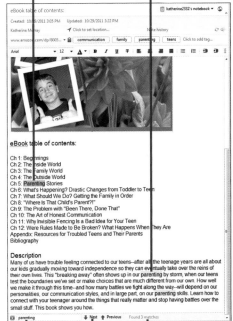

Evernote tells you how many matches are found

Searching and Replacing Note Content

Another editing task you may need to do involves searching and replacing a word or phrase in your note.

1. Display the note in which you want to replace content.

2. Click Edit to open the Edit menu.

3. Point to Find and Replace.

4. Click Replace Within Note. The Find and Replace text boxes appear at the bottom of the note panel.

5. Click in the Find box and type the word or phrase you want to find.

6. Click in the Replace box and type the word or phrase you want to use to replace the search text.

7. If you want the search results to match the case of the text you entered, click the Match Case checkbox.

8. Click Replace. Evernote locates the first occurrence of the text you entered and replaces it with the word or phrase you specified.

Replace It All with One Fell Swoop

If you want to replace every instance of a particular phrase—for example, perhaps you misspelled a team member's name or you got a product name wrong—you can enter the text you want to find and the text you want to use to replace it, and then click Replace All. Evernote will make all the exchanges for you in one pass. Nice.

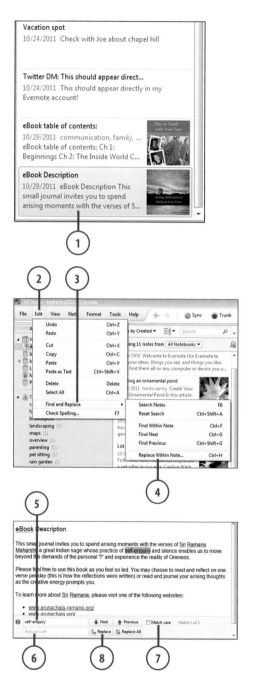

Changing the Font, Size, and Style of Text

You may select the font you use in your notes for its functionality—*how many words can I cram on this page?*—for its personality (purple! OVERSIZED! Or *italicized*). You may use all kinds of fonts, sizes, and styles, or you might use just one. You can set the font choices you prefer as you create a new note, or you can go back and make all these changes later if you prefer.

Choosing a New Font

The type family you choose for your note conveys a particular kind of tone in your notes. For a playful note, you might use Kristen ITC. For a more serious note you share with others, you might use Times New Roman

Changing the font is simple in Evernote, and it basically involves just selecting the text you want to change and making a new selection.

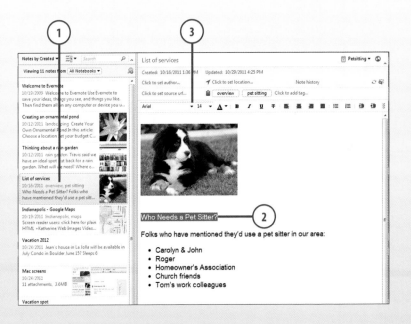

1. Click the note you want to change.

2. Highlight the text for which you want to change the font.

3. Click the Font arrow.

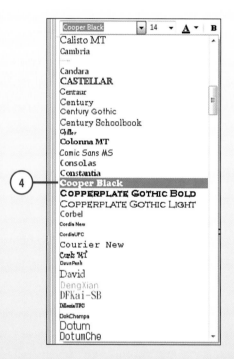

4. Click the name of the font you want to apply to the selected text.

Let's See Those Fonts

Press ⌘+T to show all the fonts available to you as you use Evernote on your Mac.

Two- or Four-Faced Fonts?

You might notice that the fonts you select for your notes are a bit slippery, depending on which platform you're using to view the notes you create. If you choose Arial 12 pt on your desktop machine and then view that same note on your Android phone, it can look much different. Some of this might be due to the font you've set as the default on your device, and some might be due to an as-yet unresolved inconsistency in Evernote. You might not always get the fonts you expect, but hopefully this will be fixed in a future Evernote update.

Changing Text Size

Changing the size of the text in your notes is likewise an easy task. You may want to enlarge the size of text when you want it to serve as a heading; you might shrink text when you want it to appear as a footnote.

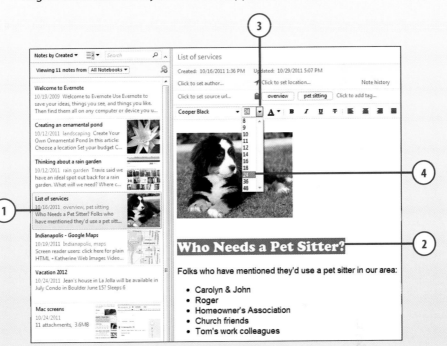

1. Display the note with the text you want to change.

2. Select the text you want to resize.

3. Click the Size arrow.

4. Click the size you want to apply to the text.

Quickly Changing Font Size

You can quickly increase or decrease text one size on the Mac by pressing ⌘++(plus) to make the text bigger or pressing ⌘+- (minus) to make the text one size smaller.

Supersize Windows Text Size

You can boost (or shrink) text on your Windows PC by pressing Ctrl+[to enlarge the text or Ctrl+] to make it smaller. Each time you press the shortcut key, Evernote bumps the text size one size up or down, depending on which shortcut key you use.

Selecting a New Text Style

The style of text makes it easy for you to add a little flavor to your text. You might **shout something boldly** or *lean in to emphasizing something* or <u>underline something that's really important</u>.

1. Display the note you want to change.

2. Select the text to which you want to apply the style(s).

3. Click the style in the editing toolbar you want to apply.

Windows Style Shortcut Keys

Here are a few shortcut keys for quick style changes on your Windows PC: Highlight the text you want to change and press Ctrl+B for **bold**, Ctrl+I for *italic*, Ctrl+U for <u>underlined</u> text, and Ctrl+T for ~~strikethrough~~ text.

The Mac Approach to Style Shortcuts

If you want to take a shortcut for style on your Mac, press ⌘+B for **bold**, ⌘+I for *italic*, and ⌘+U for <u>underlined</u> text.

GOING STYLE-LESS

>>> Go Further

You can do away with the formatting altogether by selecting the text you want to return to an *au naturale* state and pressing Ctrl+spacebar on your Windows PC.

You might also want to paste information from another program but not bring the formatting styles along with the content you're pasting. Suppose, for example, that you are dragging a highlighted list from a Word document but you don't want either the bullets or the highlighting to appear in your Evernote note. You can copy the information from the Word document, and then press Ctrl+Shift+V on your Windows PC keyboard or ⌘+up arrow+V on your Mac to paste the text on the note page without formatting.

Working with Text Color

Isn't it nice to have the option of working with color as you're collecting and organizing your notes? You might use color as a way to earmark certain types of content—for example, coloring all your notes about recycling green or your notes about an upcoming trip purple. Or perhaps you just like to have some variety and like to assign different colors to different notes. Whatever your approach, Evernote makes applying color to your notes simple.

Changing the Color of Text

When you want to change the color of text you've entered, you can select the text and choose a new color. If you want to enter text in a new color, you can click to anchor the cursor, choose a new color, and then enter the text normally.

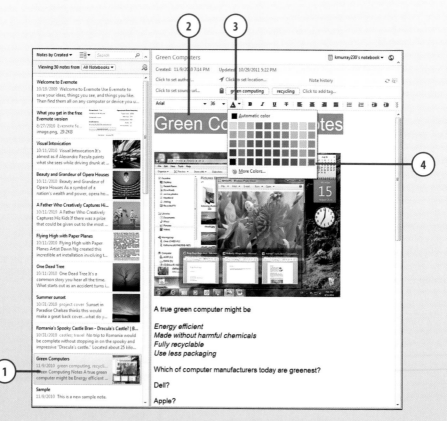

1. Select the note with the text you want to change.

2. Highlight the text.

3. Click the Text Color tool to display the color palette.

4. Click the color you want to apply.

Keeping Incoming Formats

If you are copying text from another program that was in a second color, Evernote will automatically keep the color format.

Choosing a Custom Color

You can create your own custom color to match other items you may use in your business or project. Suppose, for example, that you use a specific color scheme for your logo and letterhead. You can customize the text in your Evernote notes to have that same exact color scheme by creating custom color with the same values as the colors you use in your other documents.

1. Select the note with the text you want to change.

2. Select the text you want to change.

3. Click the Text Color tool in the editing toolbar.

4. Click More Colors. The Color dialog box appears.

5. Click Define Custom Colors.

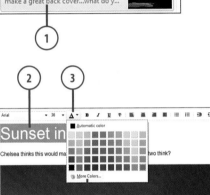

Any custom colors you create appear in, and are selectable from, these boxes.

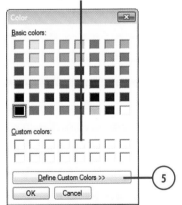

6. Click to choose a new custom color.

7. Adjust the color as needed using the vertical slider.

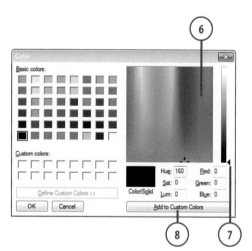

What Is RGB?

No, it's not a secret service organization. RGB stands for Red, Green, Blue, and it refers to the values used to make up a specific shade of a color you use in your printed or electronic materials. When you create a custom color in Evernote, you can choose the RGB values for the hue, and this helps you ensure that the color you choose is consistent.

8. Click Add to Custom Colors. The new color is added to the Custom Colors area at the bottom of the Colors dialog box so that you can easily choose it when you want to add custom colors to your notes.

>>> Go Further

CHANGING COLORS ON YOUR MAC

If you want to choose a custom color for note text in Evernote for Mac, begin by selecting the text and then clicking the Color tool in the toolbar just above the note area. The Colors dialog box appears. Click the color you want to apply, and click the Color Sliders tool to adjust the color attributes. You can click Color Palettes to choose from a range of color palettes (existing palettes include Apple, the default selection, Web Safe Colors, Crayons, and Developer), or click the tool to the right of the Palette list to create a new palette or open an existing one not already displayed.

Clicking Image Palettes at the top of the Colors dialog box displays a spectrum of color available in the selected palette; and clicking Crayons displays—you guessed it—a set of crayons in the colors you'd expect to see in your favorite box of crayons. For each of these color selections, you can click your selection to apply it to the selected text.

Aligning and Indenting Your Text

The position of the text on your Evernote page can help you call attention to content in your notes or find specific items easily later. Evernote's alignment and indent features are simple to use. You'll find them in the Format menu, and they are also available when you highlight text in the note and right-click to display the context menu.

You'll find the tools you need in the editing toolbar of the note window. Each tool shows you how the text will be aligned after you click the tool:

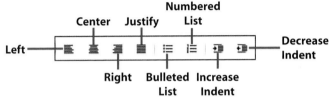

Aligning Your Text

Evernote makes it easy for you to align the text in your notes as you would like it to appear. The text is aligned along the left margin by default, but you can also choose center, right, or justified alignment. Center, of course, centers the text on the page; right aligns the text along the right margin of the note; and justified aligns text along both the left and right margin by adding space between the words in the line.

1. Display the note with the text you want to change.

2. Select the text.

3. Click the alignment tool in the editing toolbar that reflects the way you want the text to be formatted.

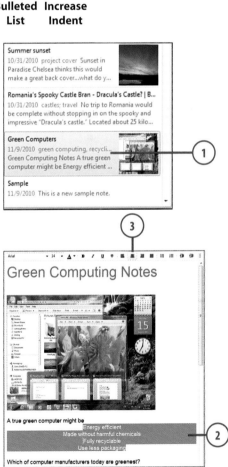

Working with Text Indents

You can easily indent the text in your notes to call attention to specific passages or help blocks of text catch your reader's eye. Or maybe you just want to change the indent of text because you want to be able to find it again easily later when you scan through your notes.

1. Select the note with the text you want to change.

2. Highlight the text.

3. Click either the Increase Indent or Decrease Indent tool. The text moves in the direction you select.

Flush Left

The Decrease Indent tool is available only after you have previously used Increase Indent. In other words, you must move the text to the right before you'll be able to use Decrease Indent to move text back out toward the left margin.

Indenting Lists

You can also apply indents to your bulleted and numbered lists. When you click the Format menu, point to Paragraph, and choose Increase Indentation or Decrease Indentation, the bullet or numbered list moves to the right or left as you select.

Creating Lists

Lists, lists, lists. Where would we be without bulleted or numbered lists? Books like this one would be a long, confusing paragraph of non-differentiated steps. (Read: nightmare!) Evernote knows that you want to put your notes in lists to make them as easy as possible to scan and follow.

Use bulleted lists when you want to show a number of items but they can appear in any particular order (for example, a book list your students can use to choose the one they want to write a report about). Numbered lists are typically used when you want to share information that needs to be done in order—such as the steps for the tasks in this book, a list providing instructions on how to bake homemade bread, or a list that tells people how to apply for a scholarship.

Adding a Bulleted List

Lists in Evernote are straightforward, without a lot of bells and whistles. You can create a list and add bullets, and that's about it. No fancy bullets, no alternate characters. You can't even change the color of the always-black bullet character.

1. Choose the note you want to format.

2. Highlight the text you want to turn into a bulleted list.

3. Click the Bulleted List tool.

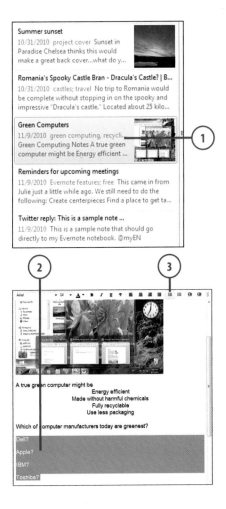

ADDING COLOR TO BULLETS

Even though Evernote doesn't allow you to change the color of bullets you create on your notes pages, you can import color from an outside program, such as Microsoft Word. If you create a bulleted list in Word, for example, with red bullet characters, when you copy and paste the list into Evernote, the bullets will retain their color. Unfortunately, if you also change the bullet character, perhaps using a special symbol as the bullet in your list, the character won't make it to your Evernote pages—Evernote will exchange the custom bullet with a traditional one, even though it will retain the color you've applied.

Creating a Numbered List

Creating a numbered list is similar to creating a bulleted list. You add the items you want to include in the list and click the Numbered List tool.

1. Choose the note you want to format.

2. Highlight the text you want to format as a numbered list.

3. Click the Numbered List tool in the editing toolbar.

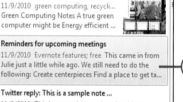

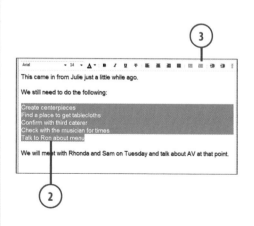

It's Not All Good

Not So Simple Simplifying

Evernote also includes an option called Simplify Formatting, available in the Tools menu. The idea here is to reduce the number of formatting styles used in your document so the note takes up less room and is easier to manage. The problem is that Simplify Formatting occasionally simplifies your note so much that it disappears completely. If your note goes missing after you use Simplify Formatting, you can click Note History to retrieve the most recent version if you're a Premium user. If you're using the free version of Evernote, you might just want to avoid Simplify Formatting.

Adding a Table to Your Note

Adding notes freeform works great, especially if you are operating in stream-of-consciousness mode or you're using ink to add your notes to the page. But what about those times when you want to compare two items—for example, weighing out a site you're considering for an upcoming meeting? If you had a list of details about each site, such as number of occupants the meeting room holds, how much the rental costs, what kind of audio-visual equipment is available, and who you need to contact, lining up the information side by side so that you could see which one looks better on paper would be helpful, right?

That's what tables are all about on your Evernote pages. Tables can help you see at a glance how two or more items compare in your notes, which can help you get closer toward a decision that's been dogging you for a while. Nice.

Creating a New Table

Before you create your table, thinking through how you want to contrast the information you'll add to it is a good idea. This helps you decide what to put in the columns, and what to put in the rows. For example, if you're comparing event meeting sites, you might use the columns for the different meeting choices, and use the rows to list the characteristics of each—size of room, number of occupants, rental cost, and so on.

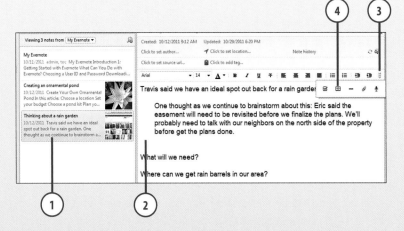

1. Click the note where you want to add the table.

2. Click to position the mouse cursor on the note.

3. Click the More button at the right end of the editing toolbar.

4. Click the Insert Table tool. The Insert Table palette appears.

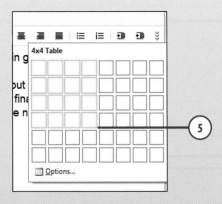

5. Drag to select the number of rows and columns you want to create.

Travis said we have an ideal spot out back for a rain garden.

One thought as we continue to brainstorm about this: Eric said the easement will need to be revisited before we finalize the plans. We'll probably need to talk with our neighbors on the north side of the property before get the plans done.

Location	Pond Style	Pond Size	Description
North			

(6)

What will we need?

Where can we get rain barrels in our area?

6. Enter the first column header and press Tab. Continue entering the table text, pressing Tab after each entry.

Modifying the Table

It's not unusual for tables to grow as we work with them. Suppose that you've created a table with four columns and five rows. Suddenly, you think of another item you need to add as a row. No problem. You can easily add or remove rows and columns while you're working with tables in Evernote.

1. Display the note containing the table you want to change.

Notes by Created ▼   Search

Viewing 3 notes from My Evernote ▼

My Evernote
10/11/2011 admin, toc My Evernote Introduction 1: Getting Started with Evernote What Can You Do with Evernote? Choosing a User ID and Password Downloadi...

Creating an ornamental pond
10/12/2011 Create Your Own Ornamental Pond In this article: Choose a location Set your budget Choose a pond kit Plan yo...

Thinking about a rain garden
10/12/2011 Travis said we have an ideal spot out back for a rain garden. One thought as we continue to brainstorm a...

(1)

2. Right-click the table row or column where you want to modify the table. A context menu appears offering choices for table changes:

- Click **Insert Row Above** to add a full row above the cursor position.

- Click **Insert Row Below** to insert a row below the cursor position.

- Click **Insert Column to the Left** to add a new column to the left of the cursor position.

- Click **Insert Column to the Right** to add a new column to the right of the cursor position.

- Choose **Delete Row** if you want to remove the current row.

- Choose **Delete Column** if you want to remove the column where the cursor is positioned.

Travis said we have an ideal spot out back for a rain garden.

One thought as we continue to brainstorm about this: Eric said the easement will need to be revisited before we finalize the plans. We'll probably need to talk with our neighbors on the north side of the property before get the plans done.

Location	Pond Style	Pond Size	Description
North	Oval	6'	Small lotus pond
South			Med koi pond
West			Med plant pond

Insert Row Above
Insert Row Below
Insert Column to the Left
Insert Column to the Right
Delete Row
Delete Column

What will

Where c   area?

(2)

INSERTING A HORIZONTAL RULE

>> Go Further

A simple way to add a little organization to your note text is inserting a divider line. This simple line is nothing fancy, but it helps you see where one topic ends and another begins, and you can use the line as creatively as you like in your Evernote notes.

To add a divider line to your note page, click to position the cursor where you want the line to appear. Then click the More button at the end of the editing tools row and click the Horizontal Rule tool. You can also insert the line using the menu, if you prefer, by clicking the Format menu and choosing Insert Horizontal Rule.

Creating a To-Do List

I come from a long line of listmakers. Let's see—what's on the agenda today? Take clothes to the cleaners. Check. Buy groceries for dinner. Check. A meeting about a new project, 10:00 a.m. Check.

If life makes more sense to you when you have a To-Do list to complete, you'll love the checklist feature in Evernote. You can create—and check off!—items on the Evernote page so that you know what you need to accomplish and can have the satisfaction of crossing an item off your list when you're done.

Adding a Check List

The process of creating a checklist isn't much different from writing a simple bullet list. You begin with the items in mind that you want to include, create the list, and add the check boxes.

1. Create a new note or select the note in which you want to add the check list.

2. Create the list you want to use as the basis for the check list.

3. Click to position the cursor at the left margin for the first item on the list.

4. Click the More button at the right end of the editing tools.

5. Click the Check Box tool. The check box is added to the list item. Repeat to add check boxes to all items on the list.

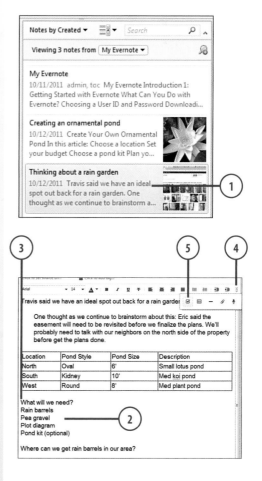

Quick Check Boxes

A fast way to add checkboxes for your to do list on your Windows PC is to position the cursor where you want to add the box and press Ctrl+Shift+C.

Check Box Tools for Mac

Unfortunately, there isn't an easy shortcut key for adding checkboxes on the Mac, but you'll find the checkbox tool in the toolbar at the top of the selected note window.

Using the To-Do List

After you have the checklist created, you can check off the items as you finish them by following these simple steps.

1. Display the note containing the check boxes.

2. Click the check box of the item you want to mark as complete.

Wiping Out the List

When you go to add check boxes to your list of options, avoid the temptation to select the entire list and add check boxes all at once. If you do this, the entire list will be replaced with a single check box. If this happens, don't panic—just press Ctrl+Z to undo your last action, click to position the cursor in front of one of the list items, and press Ctrl+Shift+C (for Windows) to add the check boxes, one at a time.

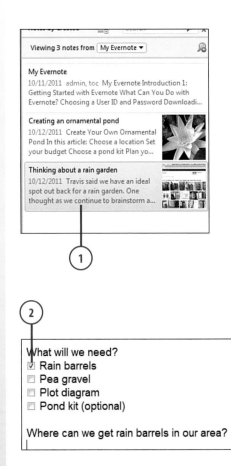

Merging Notes

Especially if you're working on a large project, you may find the number of notes you're collecting unwieldy. If you're working in a shared notebook and four or five of you are dumping notes into the shared space—wow, that's a lot of notes! Luckily, Evernote for Windows gives you a way to merge notes into a single note to make finding similar subjects easier. You can begin by locating the notes you want to combine and then select and merge them. Here's how.

1. In the Evernote notes area, select two or more notes that you want to combine.

Selecting Multiple Notes

If you want to choose more than one note in the notes list in the center of the Evernote window, press and hold Ctrl while you click the notes you want to select.

2. Click Note to open the Note menu.

3. Click Merge Notes. Evernote combines the notes and adds a new heading with the author name displayed prominently at the top. If you scroll down through the merged note you will clearly see where the second note begins.

Displaying Merge Choices

🍎 Using a Mac, you'll need to select the notes you want to merge and then Control-Click to display the Options menu. Click Merge Notes to add the notes together.

Merging Mac Notes

🍎 You can merge notes quickly on the Mac by selecting the notes you want to merge and pressing ⌘+up arrow+M.

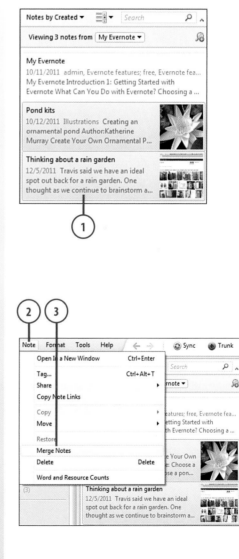

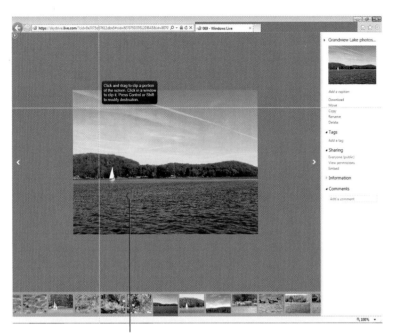

You can easily capture images
to include in your notes

You can open, edit, and save images
after you add them to your notes

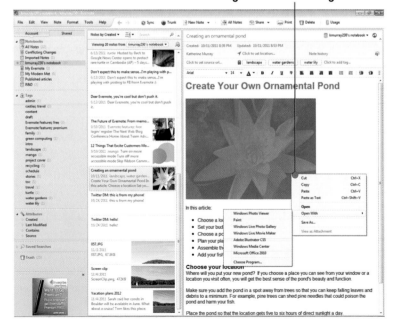

Capture interesting images—from your camera, PC, or web browser—and drag them to your notes page for extra inspiration. In this chapter, you learn to add and work with pictures in your notes by completing the following tasks:

→ Adding an Image to a Note
→ Scanning Directly into Evernote
→ Working with Images in Evernote
→ Using Skitch with Mac Images

5

Adding and Working with Images

You might start off by thinking you'll use Evernote to capture bits of text or clippings from the web that you want to add to your notebooks, but chances are that soon you'll be thinking in pictures. Images add important information to your notes, reminding you of styles you like, showing you products you're considering, displaying the diagram someone drew on the board, or capturing a photo moment that encapsulates something you want to remember about an event or story.

In this chapter you find out more about adding images to Evernote on both PC and Mac computers. You'll also get tips for sending photos from your phone, attached to the notes you collect.

THINKING OUTSIDE THE (TEXT) BOX

If you're not necessarily a visual person, you might want to brainstorm a little about how you might use images in Evernote. People tend to learn quickly from images; images, after all, can show us at a glance what may take us a paragraph (or more) to describe. Depending on what you use your notebooks to do, you might collect pictures to catalog products, show examples of designs you like, identify team members, give your team members a sense of the room you'll all be meeting in, capture the new organization chart you've been developing, get a picture of the scribbles you added to your napkin, and more. Take a few moments and think about how capturing an image—from the web, on your camera, or on your phone—can help you collect information that can be helpful to you later.

You might, for example, take pictures of books in bookstores that you want to research online, snap photos of QR codes for items you'd like to learn more about, scan instruction manuals for shop tools, capture pictures or scans of receipts, or even grab a quick photo of a service vehicle you see on the road when you don't have the time to scribble down the phone number.

Adding an Image to a Note

When you want to add an image to your Evernote note, whether you're working on your PC or Mac system or sending a note from your mobile phone, you have a number of simple ways to do that. On your desktop version of Evernote, you can simply drag and drop an image from your computer to your Evernote note. If you're using a Mac, you can use iSight to capture a live image for a notebook page. If you're using your phone, you can attach an image to an email message and email the note to your Evernote notebook. All notes are synchronized among your favorite devices so that when you log in, your up-to-date notes are reflected on your PC, on the web, and on your phone.

Dragging and Dropping Images

The easiest way to add images to your notes in Evernote is to simply drag and drop the image you want to use into a new note window.

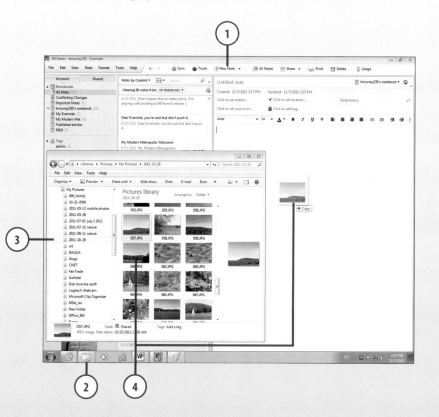

1. Click New Note. The new note window opens.

2. Click the Windows Explorer icon in the taskbar.

3. Click to choose the folder containing the image you want to add to the note.

4. Drag the image to the note page and release the mouse button.

Finishing the Note

When you drag and drop an image to a new note, Evernote automatically assigns the photo's filename to the note title. You can change the title by clicking in the title at the top of the note and typing a new title. You can also set all the note properties and add text to the note as needed.

Drag-and-Drop Magic

On your Mac, you can drag and drop an image to your Evernote notebook easily by simply dragging it to the Evernote icon in the Dock. Evernote will automatically create a new note in your default notebook and you can go back later, if you like, and add text to expand the note content.

Attaching Images to Messages

Another way to add images to your Evernote notes involves attaching pictures to email messages you send using your Evernote address. Whether you're emailing from your phone, from another computer, or from a web kiosk somewhere on a cruise ship in the Mediterranean, you can easily add an image and send it directly to Evernote, for easy retrieval later.

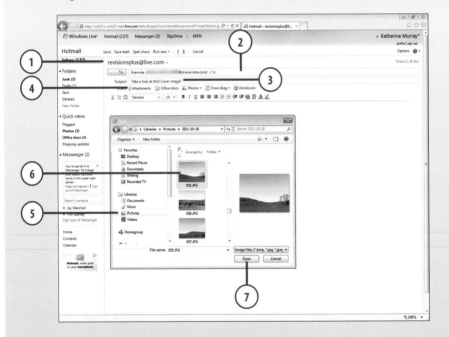

1. Open your email program and start a new message.

2. Enter your Evernote email address in the To line.

3. Type a subject for the message.

4. Click the Attachments link.

5. Click the folder in which the picture is stored.

6. Click the image you want to attach.

7. Click Open. The image file is added to the message.

8. Enter the text you want to send with the message.

9. Click Send. The email is sent to your Evernote account and is saved as a new note in your default notebook.

Photos, Too

In Windows Live Hotmail, you can add photos by using either the Attachments tool or the Photos tool in the Insert line. When you click Attachments, you can choose from among files stored on your computer. If you have photos stored in web albums online or you want to search for images available on the web, click Photos and choose the photo you want to send.

Adding Images with iSight

 If you're using a Mac to gather your Evernotes, you have an additional image-capturing option for plunking pictures directly in your new note window. A tool called iSight is displayed at the top of the Evernote for Mac window. You can click that tool to take a picture of yourself in all your loveliness. Of course, you can also hold up a chart, show a book title, or display whatever you want (keep it clean) for your Mac camera capture enjoyment. The image is added automatically to your new note and filed away in your handy-dandy notebook.

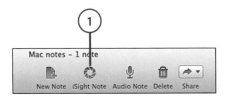

1. Click iSight Note.

2. Display the picture you want to capture. Click Take Photo Snapshot. iSight displays a red bar with a countdown so that you have time to smile for the camera.

3. If you want to Discard the image you captured and close iSight, click Discard.

4. To save the image you captured to your note page, click Add to Evernote.

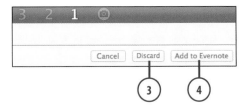

Moving the Image to Another Note

If you accidentally add your iSight screen capture to the wrong note, you can select and drag it to the note on which you want it to appear.

Capturing Windows Screens

⊞ Evernote for Windows comes with a utility that Evernote calls the "Evernote Helper," but good luck if you go looking for it where they say it can be found—in your system tray, close to the clock on your PC. Instead you need to use the shortcut key combination to activate the screen clipping utility. You'll also notice that it changes the way Windows normally works—that is, the PrintScreen key takes on a slightly different personality when the Evernote Helper comes into play.

1. Display the screen that you want to capture for your Evernote note.

2. Press and hold the Windows key and press PrintScreen. This key combination starts screen capture mode in Evernote. A crosshair appears on your screen.

3. Click and drag a segment of the window. Evernote puts that area of the screen in a new note and displays it in the preview panel on the right side of the Evernote window.

4. In Evernote, click in the note header at the top of the window to add a note title.

5. Add note properties as desired.

6. Enter note text to complete the note.

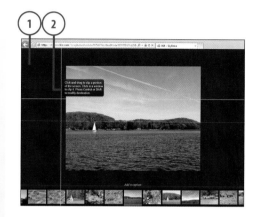

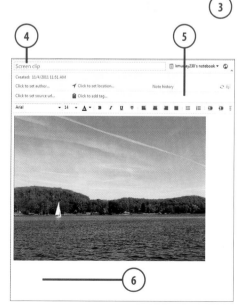

Capturing the Whole Screen

If you are running the Evernote Helper and you want to capture the entire screen and put it in a new Evernote note, press Windows key+PrintScreen and then click anywhere in the window you want to capture. The whole screen is captured and appears in the note. If you want to capture only one open window (for example, perhaps you are viewing the contents of a folder you'd like to take a screen capture of), press the Windows key and press PrintScreen and click that window. That window will be captured and pasted into the Evernote note.

WINDOWS SCREEN CAPTURE SHORTCUT KEYS

To Do This	Follow This Action
Copy the clipped image to the Windows clipboard	Press Windows key+PrintScreen; then press Ctrl while dragging.
Save the clipped image to your Windows desktop	Press Windows key+PrintScreen; then press Shift while dragging.
Copy the clipped image to a new Evernote note	Press Windows key+PrintScreen; click and drag the portion of the screen you want to capture.

Scanning Directly into Evernote

As a collector of information, Evernote makes gathering up stray bits and pieces of data you've scattered around in various places easy for you. You can clip things from the web, tweet notes to yourself, send email directly to your notebook, capture pictures of doodles and designs you like, and even scan documents and photos directly into Evernote.

Some scanners enable you to scan the image directly into an Evernote folder, and other scanners require that you set the Evernote email address up as the recipient of the scan. This section shows you a couple of ways you can scan your content into Evernote.

Content Is Content Is Content

Note that after your scanner is working with Evernote, you can scan either images or text notes—or other things, such as awards, ribbons, and other embellishments—to your notes.

Emailing to Evernote

Evernote gives you a unique email address to use if you want to email things to your Evernote account. You can enter that address to the settings of your printer/scanner to have the scanned item sent directly to your Evernote account. To find your Evernote email address, click Tools and click Account Info. You'll find your email address in the Email Notes To line of the information in the Account Info dialog box. Right-click it and choose Copy if you want to copy and paste it into the appropriate field in your scanning software.

Setting Up Your Scanner

First things first. To get your scanner talking directly to Evernote, you begin with your scanner software and plug in the right settings. If your scanner is one that works seamlessly with Evernote (lucky you—see the later table), you can choose Evernote as the choice in the Scan To field. If Evernote doesn't work directly with your scanner (which is the case for me), you can use the Evernote email address to send the scanned image or document directly to your Evernote account.

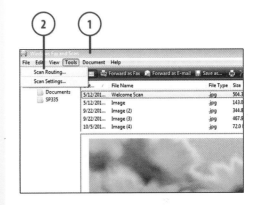

1. Turn on your scanner and start your scanning program (in this case, I've used Windows Fax and Scan).

2. Find the option that controls the routing of the items you scan. In Windows Fax and Scan, click Tools and click Scan Routing.

3. If necessary, click an option that tells the scanning utility to send the scanned image by email.

4. Enter the email address to your Evernote account.

5. Enter other options, such as the phrase you want to appear in the From entry on the email message.

6. Enter the server name your email account uses to send email. You'll find this value by clicking File in Outlook 2010, clicking Account Settings, double-clicking your email address, and looking for the value in the Outgoing mail server (SMTP) box.

7. Enter the Outgoing server or port information. Find this information by clicking the More Settings button in the Outlook 2010 Internet E-mail Settings window and clicking the Advanced tab. The number you want appears in the Outgoing server (SMTP) box.

8. Click Save.

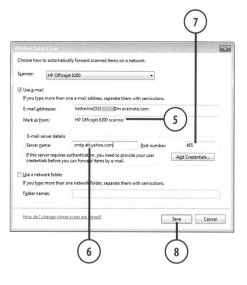

ADJUSTING SCANNER SETTINGS FOR EVERNOTE FOR THE MAC

With Evernote for the Mac, you can choose to scan directly to Evernote—no email address needed. Begin by launching your scanning utility.

In the settings dialog for your scanner (such as an HP Officejet 6200), click the Show Details button. In the settings dialog that appears, click the Scan To arrow. A pop-up list appears, offering you a range of choices. Click Other and then choose Applications. A list of your current applications appears. Scroll down to display Evernote, and click Choose. Now, back in the scanning window, click Scan to scan the image directly to Evernote.

>>> Go Further

SCANNING DIRECTLY TO EVERNOTE

Scanner	Description
Canon ImageFormula P-150	Scans your content directly into Evernote
Doxie Scanner	A small portable scanner that scans anything, anywhere—no computer needed—and then syncs directly to Evernote
Fujitsu ScanSnap	Scans receipts, business cards, and documents
Lexmark SmartSolution Printers	Scans all content you want to include in Evernote

Scanning on Your iPhone

If you're using an iPhone, you can download an app called DocScanner to scan images directly into your Evernote account. DocScanner has a QuickScan option that enables you to scan the photo or page and send it easily from your phone. Check the Mac App Store for more information.

Scanning into Evernote

When you are ready to scan something directly into Evernote, you simply start your scanning software as you normally would and scan the image or file you want to include in your notes. This example uses Windows Fax and Scan, but after you've set up your scanner to send the scanned image directly to Evernote—either by email or by direct scanning—you can use any scanning utility you like.

1. Start your scanning utility. Begin by clicking Start.

2. Type Windows Fax and Scan in the search box.

3. Click the utility name to launch the program.

4. Place the image you want to scan picture side down in your scanner, and click New Scan.

5. Click the Color Format arrow to choose the Color format you want to use. Typically scanners offer Color, Grayscale, and Black and White choices.

6. Click the File Type arrow to choose the file type you want to use for the scanned file. Most scanners enable you to choose BMP, JPG, PNG, or TIF as the output format.

7. Change the Brightness and Contrast settings if you want to enhance the image as you scan it.

8. Click Preview.

9. Drag the selection handle to resize the scanned area so that it includes only the image area you want to scan.

10. Click Scan.

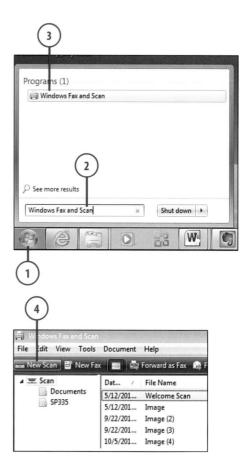

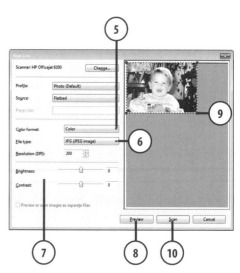

Search Text in Your Scanned Images

Evernote scans the content of both images and text files so that any text in the scanned document can be searched. You may notice a difference in how quickly this happens—Premium users will find that their files have been scanned and are searchable more quickly (in just a few hours) than free account users.

Working with Images in Evernote

After you've added images to your note pages, that's not all there is. You can still work with images if you like, by copying and pasting them to other notes, opening them in your favorite image editor and modifying them, and saving them as files you can use in other places as well.

Copying and Pasting an Image

In Evernote for Windows, you can easily move images from note to note in Evernote, or copy and paste the same image among a number of different notes. Here's how.

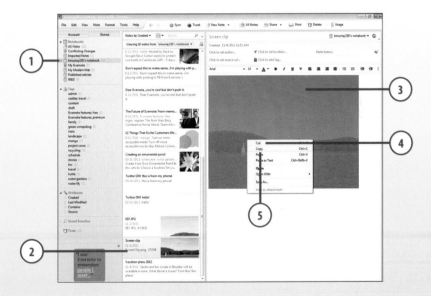

1. Click the notebook you want to use.
2. Click to select the note that includes the image you want to copy.
3. Right-click the image. A context menu appears, offering you a number of options.
4. If you want to remove the image from the note and place a copy of it on the clipboard, click Cut.
5. If you want to create a copy of the image, click Copy.

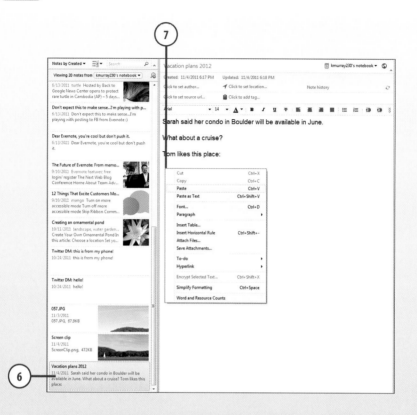

6. Select the note where you want to paste the copied or cut image. You can also start a new note if you like by clicking New Note at the top of the Evernote window.

7. Right-click at the point in the note where you want to add the image and select Paste.

Undoing Your Addition

You can quickly remove an image you didn't mean to add by pressing Ctrl+Z to undo your last action.

Opening an Image for Editing

The image that you add to your Evernote page may not be in great shape. Maybe the shadows are too dark or other items are in the picture that you don't want to show. You can do simple edits by opening the image in Evernote. Evernote lets you choose among the image editing programs you have installed on your computer to do the work.

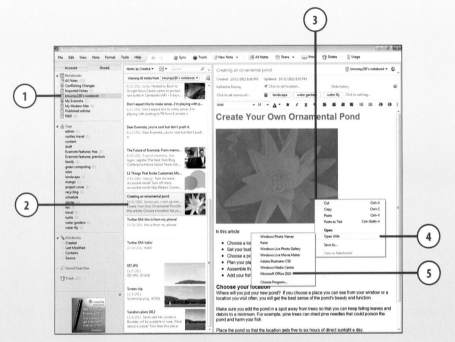

1. Click the notebook containing the note you want to use.

2. Click the note with the image you want to open.

3. Right-click the image to display the context menu.

4. Point to Open With. A list of image editing or graphics programs installed on your computer appears.

5. Click the name of the program you want to use. In this example, Microsoft Office 2010 opens the Microsoft Office 2010 Picture Manager, which you can use to edit, adjust, crop, and resize the selected image.

Making Simple Image Changes

Some of the image choices you see when you click Open With may be utilities that enable you to view your pictures; others give you options for editing images. If you click Microsoft Office 2010, for example, and you have the suite installed on your Windows computer, Evernote opens the picture in Microsoft Office 2010 Picture Manager. No matter which image editing tool you use, the steps you follow will be similar to the ones shown here.

1. In your image editor, use the editing tools to make the adjustments you want to make.

2. Use the Auto Correct feature to balance the color and brightness automatically.

3. Click Resize to change the size of the image.

4. Use Crop to crop unwanted elements out of the picture.

5. Click Save to save your editing changes.

6. Click Exit to close the image editor and return to Evernote, with your changes intact.

Editing Your Images, One at a Time

Even though you can add multiple images to a single note in Evernote, you must open and edit them one at a time. If you prefer to change the images all at once—for example, perhaps changing a set of color pictures to black and white—you can use a batch utility in some image editors to make that kind of change before you add the pictures to Evernote.

Saving the Image Outside Your Note

After you've made a few changes to the image, you may decide you want to keep a copy of the picture to use in other things. No problem—you can easily save the image as a file that you can use and share outside of your Evernote notes.

1. Click the note with the image you want to save.

2. Right-click the image on the note to open the context menu.

3. Click Save As. The Save As dialog box appears.

4. Click the Save In arrow to display and choose the folder in which you want to save the file.

5. Enter or change the name of the file, if desired.

6. Click Save.

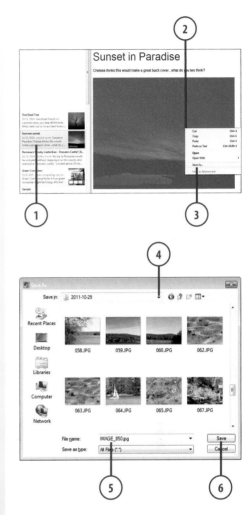

Using the Saved Image

After you save an image to a file, you can use it in any way you choose. One thing you might want to do is add it back as an attachment to a note. This helps you keep files together but it doesn't take up space within the body of the note to display the image. To add an image as an attachment, click File and click Attach Files. In the Open dialog box, navigate to the folder containing the image you want to attach, and click Open. The file is added to the note as an attachment.

Using Skitch with Mac Images

Skitch is an image add-on tool for Mac and Android Evernote users. Using Skitch, you can capture, edit, and annotate your pictures, resizing and sharing them with others using your Android phone, your iOS device, or your Mac computer. You can download Skitch from the Mac App Store or the Android Market. After you download and install the utility, launch Skitch by clicking it in your Applications folder. This loads Skitch so that it is ready to use whenever you're ready to use it.

Opening an Image in Skitch

If you want to use Skitch with an image you already have, you can simply drag it from a folder to the Skitch icon in the dock, and Skitch opens the image in the Skitch window.

1. Click the image you want to open in Skitch.

2. Drag the image to the Skitch icon in the Dock or the Skitch icon at the top of the screen, and release the mouse button.

3. Skitch opens the image in the Skitch Plus frame in the center of your desktop. Now the image is ready for editing.

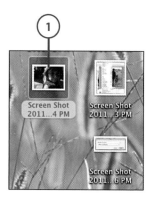

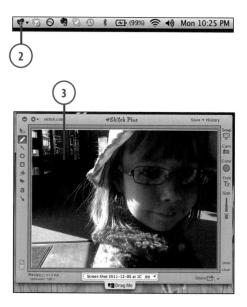

Capturing an Image in Skitch

You can also use Skitch to capture images that you have displayed on your desktop, whether you're viewing it in your browser, in iPhoto, or in one of your folders.

1. Display the image you want to capture.

2. If the image you want to capture is in your browser, click the Skitch arrow at the top of your browser window. A menu of choices appears.

3. Click the command that reflects whether you want to capture the full screen or a portion of the screen. Alternatively, you can capture an image that is on your screen using one of these shortcut keys:

    • Press Shift+⌘+5 to drag an area on the screen you want to capture.

    • Press Shift+⌘+6 to capture a full-screen shot.

    • Press Shift+⌘+7 to capture the image on your screen and display it in the Skitch frame so you can add arrows, shapes, captions, and more to the art.

After you choose how you want to capture the image, the picture is displayed in the Skitch frame so that you can edit, annotate, and share the picture with others (and with your Evernote notebook).

Editing an Image in Skitch

Skitch gives you several tools to draw, highlight, or add notes to your pictures. With Skitch, you can add notes to your images, point out important elements, or have a little fun with the images you include in your notes. Here's a quick overview of some of the things you can do with Skitch:

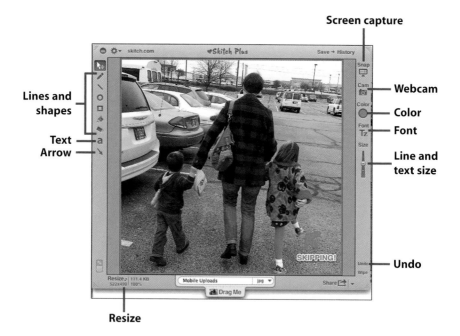

- Add lines, shapes, and colors to your image

- Insert text, such as thought bubbles or captions

- Position an arrow to point out a special element

- Resize the image

- Take a new screen capture

- Capture a picture with your webcam

- Choose the color you want to use for drawing and annotating

- Select the font used for text notes

- Choose the size of the text and shape lines

- Undo a change

Undo, Please!

You might find that at times when you try to draw something by hand, the shape or arrow looks a bit out of whack. You can remove items you don't want to keep by clicking Undo in the lower-right corner of the Skitch Plus frame. If you want to do away with all the changes you've made, click Clear.

Sharing a Skitch Image

When you've added all the notes and done all the editing you want to do, you can save your Skitch'd image and share it with your Evernote note or with others online.

1. Click the Skitch tools arrow in the upper-left corner of the Skitch frame.

2. Click Share or press ⌘+/. The first time you use Skitch, you will be prompted to log in to Evernote.

3. Click Evernote Login. The login box appears so that you can sign in.

4. Enter your username.

5. Type your password.

6. Click the Skitch Terms of Use checkbox.

7. Click Login. Skitch displays two options: You can click Image Page Link to copy the image to Evernote, or click Tweet This Image to send it to your Twitter account.

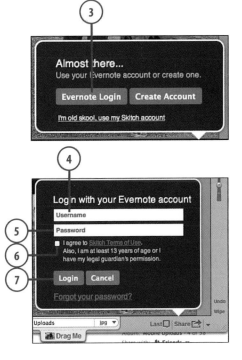

8. Click Image Page Link to send the image to Evernote.

Adding More Image Info

You also can choose the privacy setting you want to apply for the image and add a title and description if you like. Click the Details tab to add the additional information to your image before you add it to your Evernote notebook.

Evernote gives you a set of
tools you can use to add ink
notes to your notebooks

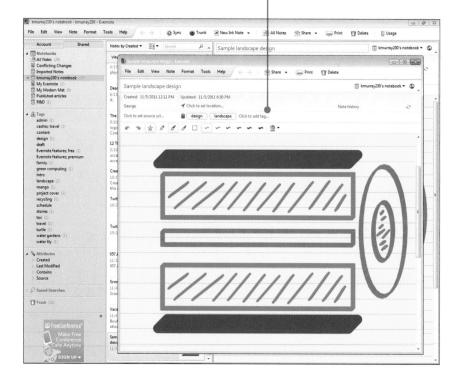

Evernote can read your handwriting too—
use the ink feature on your Windows PC or
tablet to sketch or write your notes by hand.
In this chapter, you learn how to use ink to
draw, sketch, and write your notes by completing the following tasks:

6

→ Starting an Ink Note
→ Choosing Your Pen
→ Selecting Line Style and Color
→ Inking Your Note
→ Undoing and Redoing Your Ink

Inking Your Notes

Depending on what type of note-taker you are, you may prefer to doodle and sketch your notes. If you draw organizational
charts, diagram new designs, or create drafts of illustrations
you plan to finalize later, you'll find ink notes in Evernote a nat-
ural way to capture your inspiration on the page.

Ink notes are available only in Evernote for Windows, although
both Evernote for Mac and Evernote for Android include a feature called Skitch, which enables you to add sketching and
handwritten notes to your images. You can create ink notes on
any Windows computer, whether or not you have a touch or
pen-enabled tablet or you are using a traditional Windows PC.

Inking in Evernote involves creating a new ink note and
choosing the pen tip, color, and style. This chapter shows you
how to create a new ink note and customize it the way you
want.

Starting an Ink Note

Creating an ink note in Evernote is as simple as starting any kind of new note. The difference comes in the way you add content to the note page. With ink, you will select a pen style; choose a color and thickness; and draw, sketch, or write your note on the page.

>> Go Further

CALIBRATING YOUR TABLET

If you plan to use a drawing tablet or a touch-based tablet to add ink notes in Evernote, you may want to calibrate your tablet or set up your pen and touch capabilities before you begin creating notes.

You'll find what you need in the Hardware and Sound area of the Control Panel. Click Start and then Click Control Panel. Finally, click Hardware and Sound to display your options.

In the Tablet PC Settings of the Hardware and Sound category of the Control Panel, you can configure your device so that it responds accurately to the way you use the pen or touch the screen. You can also change the settings for left- or right-handed use.

You can set up what you need for pen and touch features by clicking the Pen and Touch category. In the Pen and Touch dialog box, you can set up how you want the pen buttons to function, practice gestures such as navigational and editing flicks, and change how sensitive the device is to touch. You can also turn on automatic learning for handwriting so that Windows learns and recognizes how to read your handwriting.

Creating an Ink Note

Working with ink in Evernote makes sketching out your ideas and making them available in searches later easy. Here are the basic steps for creating your first ink note.

1. Click New Note.

2. Click New Ink Note.

3. Click the Pencil tool.

4. Click and drag on the page to draw your ink note.

Ink the Quick Way

You can also press Ctrl+Shift+I to create a new ink note in Evernote.

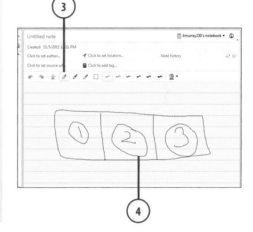

INK IS FOR WINDOWS, BUT MAC AND ANDROID HAVE SKITCH

>>> Go Further

Ink notes are available only in Evernote for Windows but if you want to annotate a picture or draw on an image on your Mac computer or Android phone, you can use Skitch. You'll find more about Skitch in Chapter 5, "Adding and Working with Images."

Skitch is an image annotation feature that makes adding handwritten and sketched notes to images simple. You can use Skitch to add thought bubbles, circle important elements, and call attention to details. You can review designs with clients, plan event seating, and resize and rotate your images in Skitch.

You can get Skitch for the Mac from the Mac App Store and Skitch for Android from the Android Market. To find out more about Skitch, visit www.skitch.com.

Navigating the Ink Window

When you add your content in the ink note window, you'll notice a number of tools that are unique to this type of note. You can use the ink tools to choose the style and size of the strokes you make, the color of the pencil lead or pen ink, and much more. You'll find the following tools in the toolbar above the ink note area:

- Undo and Redo tools enable you to reverse repeat your last ink action.

- AutoShape is a toggle tool that helps you create well-formed shapes such as rectangles, ovals, and arrows.

- The Pencil tool draws a rounded stroke in whatever color you choose.

- The Pen tool draws a sharper stroke, also in the color and thickness of your choice.

- Use the Selection tool to select an area of your drawing or the entire note.

- The Thickness palette offers a range of thicknesses for the line you draw.

- The Color palette gives you a range of choices for the lines you create.

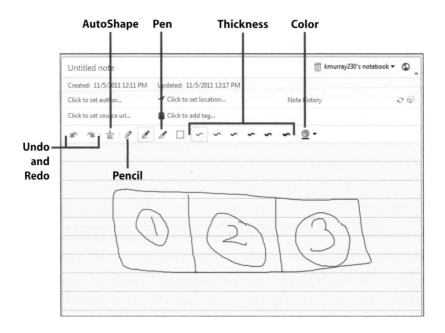

Drawing Lines and Shapes

As you learned in the last section, creating an ink note and scribbling on the page is a simple thing. You can click, drag, and be done. If you want to put a little more energy into your ink notes, you can think through what you want to show, and choose the right tool to fit the bill. You can also choose the right line thickness for the job and adjust the line color to get just the right effect.

Choosing a Tool and Setting Line Thickness

Evernote gives you two main tools for inking notes—the Pencil tool and the Pen tool. You can change the stroke of the tools to adjust their thickness and color, and each tool gives you a slightly different line.

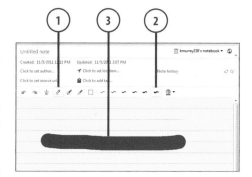

1. Click the Pencil tool.

2. Click the line thickness farthest to the right.

3. Drag to draw a line from left to right on the page.

4. Click the Pen tool.

5. Click below the first line and drag across the page. Notice that the Pen tool draws a more angled line than the pencil tool.

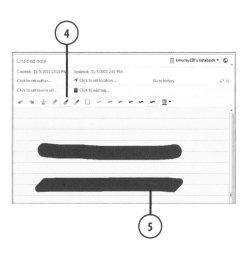

The When of Choosing Line Thickness

The inking tools in Evernote are fairly simple and straightforward, but this means they also aren't too fancy. That means that you can't change line thickness after the fact; rather, you must choose the thickness you want to use before you draw the line on the page.

You can easily clip any web
content you want to keep
using Evernote's web clippers

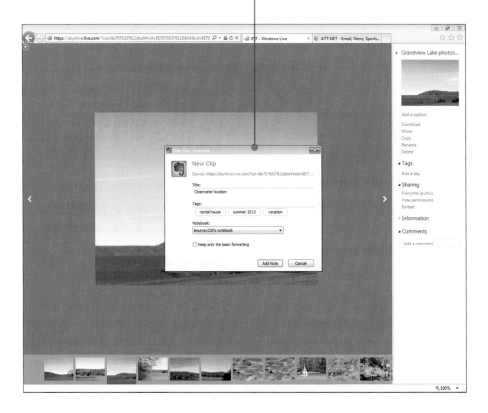

Choosing Line Color

Evernote gives you the ability to choose different colors for the notes you ink, and you can select colors from the regular color palette of you can define your own custom colors if you want to match a specific color used in your letterhead or other marketing materials.

1. Click the Pencil or Pen tool you want to use.

2. Click the thickness.

3. Click the arrow to the right of the Color tool. The Color palette appears.

4. Click the color you want to apply using the tool you selected.

5. Draw as desired on the note page to add the ink in the new color.

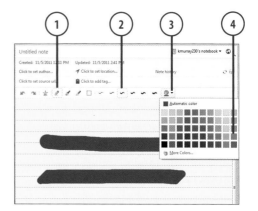

Contrasting Color

Especially if you're adding highlights, text, or boxes to images, choose a contrasting color that causes the ink to stand out against the background of the image. Vibrant red works, as does bright yellow, when you want to call attention to elements of the picture.

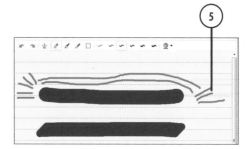

Drawing a Shape

Evernote knows that drawing a perfectly formed shape is not always easy. Perhaps you're creating an organization chart and you want to sketch in the various roles and have it look at least a little organized. Evernote's AutoShape tool takes the shapes you draw and smoothes them out so they look the way you intended them to look.

1. Click the Pen or Pencil tool.

2. Choose the line thickness.

3. Click the AutoShape tool.

4. Draw a square in the note area. When you release the mouse button, your hand-drawn shape is smoothed out and cleaned up.

5. Click the Color palette and choose a new color if you want.

6. Draw an arrow shape.

7. Change the color yet again if desired, and draw a circle.

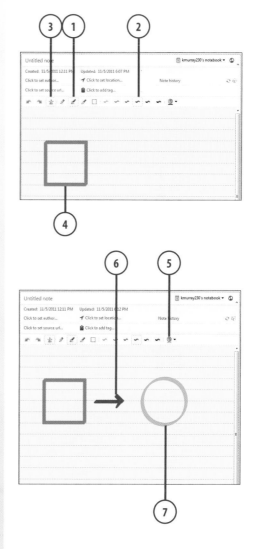

Copying, Pasting, and Moving Shapes Around

If you want to make copies of shapes or move shapes around on the Evernote note, you can use the selection tool to drag a lasso around the item you want to move and then drag it to the new location. To copy and paste a selected shape, press Ctrl+C to make the copy and Ctrl+V to paste it in a new location.

Removing Lines and Shapes

Evernote ink may be pretty basic, but it does include tools you can use to remove aspects of the ink you don't want to keep. Suppose you've drawn a landscape plan and you decide that you want to remove one section of your sketch. You can easily do this by selecting the area you want to remove or by removing individual lines.

Removing Lines

Evernote offers another tool for removing individual lines in your ink notes. You can click the Erase line tool and then click the line you want to remove from your ink note.

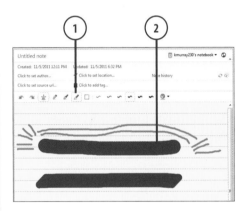

1. Click the Erase tool in the toolbar.

2. Click the line in the note you want to remove. Evernote removes the line you selected.

Deleting Shapes

When you want to remove an entire shape, the easiest way to get rid of it is to select it and delete it.

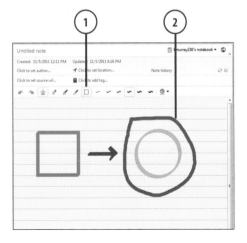

1. Click the Selection tool.

2. Drag a lasso around the shape and press Delete.

Using the Erase Tool

You can also use the Erase Tool to delete an entire shape, by clicking the tool in the toolbar and clicking the shape. The whole shape disappears. Simple.

Undoing—and Redoing—Your Actions

Finally, you can use the Undo and Redo tools to reverse your most recent actions or replace items you have undone in your ink note.

1. When you have an action you want to reverse, click Undo. Evernote reverses the actions you've previously taken.

2. If you want to replace an item you've undone or repeat your most recent action, press Redo.

Everyone Can See Ink

The ink notes you create in Evernote are converted to PNG graphics on your notes pages, so they can be searched and viewed on any device you use—Mac, Android, Blackberry, and more.

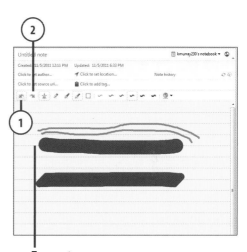

Evernote removes the most recent line you've added each time you click Undo

You can easily clip any web
content you want to keep
using Evernote's web clippers

Clip the information you find on the web and add it to your notes pages; you can also take notes using your webcam and include them in your notebooks. In this chapter, you learn how to clip notes from the web and capture your own webcam notes by completing the following tasks:

→ Setting Up the Web Clipper
→ Capturing Notes on the Web
→ Snapping a Webcam Note

Grabbing Web Clippings and Webcam Notes

As you've been learning throughout this book, Evernote makes it easy for you to grab information that inspires you and save it for later, whether you're using your PC, browser, or mobile device. Grabbing information from the web is a no-brainer; of *course* you'll find stories, pictures, designs, and more you will want to save to your note pages.

Although you can simply copy and paste information from a web page to your note, Evernote provides a tool called the *Web Clipper* that enables you to clip content and paste it directly on your pages. The great benefit here is that Evernote maintains the link to the site so that you can always go back to the site if you like or include the source URL whenever you use the information in a document or share it with others.

Setting Up the Web Clipper

Before you can get started clipping content from the web, you need to make sure the clipper is installed for your particular browser. If you're using Internet Explorer, no worries—Evernote for Windows installs the clipper automatically for you. If you're using Firefox, Safari, or Google Chrome, however, you'll need to download and install the Evernote Web Clipper for the version you use.

The process of downloading and installing the Web Clipper is similar whether you're using Safari, Firefox, or Google Chrome. In all cases, you begin at the Evernote home page by clicking Downloads and choosing the Web Clipper option. After that, Evernote recognizes which version of the clipper you need and gives you the option for downloading it.

Downloading and Installing the Firefox Web Clipper

Firefox is a free browser that is available from www.mozilla.org for Windows, Mac, and Linux computers; you can also download and use Firefox on mobile devices as well as iPhones.

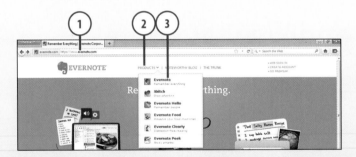

1. Launch your Firefox browser and go to the Evernote home page (www.evernote.com).

2. Click Products.

3. Click Evernote

4. Click Get the Web Clipper.

5. Click Add to Firefox.

6. When Firefox alerts you that the site wants to install software on your computer, click Allow.

7. Click the Evernote Web Clipper.

8. Click Install Now. The Web Clipper installs in your Firefox browser, and you'll see the small Evernote tool (with the elephant head logo) on the far-right end of the tools row.

EVERNOTE NEEDS YOUR COOKIES

When you install the Web Clipper in Firefox, the clipper will work properly only if you have the browser set to accept cookies from third-party sources. By default, cookies are enabled in Firefox, but if someone has changed your setting, you can change it back by clicking the Firefox button in the upper-left corner of the browser window, clicking Options, and clicking the Privacy category.

Next, in the Firefox Will list, choose Use Custom Settings for History. Then, click to add a check mark to the Accept Cookies from Sites checkbox, and click to check mark the Accept Third-Party Cookies checkbox.

In the Keep Until setting, you can decide to keep cookies until they expire or until you close Firefox (which removes the cookies after your current browsing session ends), or you can decide whether you want to accept each cookie on a case-by-case basis. (Firefox will prompt you when a site attempts to add a cookie to your browser.) Click OK to save your settings.

Downloading and Installing the Google Chrome Clipper

Google Chrome is a popular free browser from—you guessed it—Google (www.google.com/chrome) that also supports PCs, Macs, and Linux machines. Google Chrome has a minimalist design and claims to make your browsing experience fast, safe, and easy.

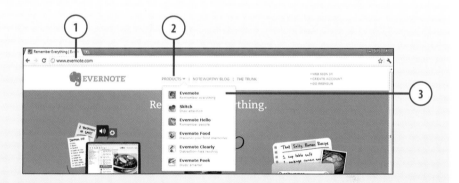

1. Launch your Google Chrome browser and display Evernote's home page (www.evernote.com).

2. Click Products.

3. Click Evernote.

4. Click Get Web Clipper. Or, if your version of Chrome installed automatically with your Windows download, you'll see Clipper Installed. If you click Get Web Clipper, the Clip to Evernote page appears, explaining more about the Evernote extension in Google Chrome.

5. Click Add to Chrome. The Install Clip to Evernote? message box appears.

6. Click Install, and the Evernote Web Clipper installs in your Google Chrome browser.

Different Clippers, Different Features

So Evernote covers a lot of ground, creating a variety of clippers for different browsers. Although the clippers are similar for Internet Explorer, Safari, Google Chrome, and Firefox, each clipper functions slightly differently from the others. Whether the clipper is installed as part of the Evernote version you downloaded (which is the case with Evernote for Windows) or you need to download and add it separately (as you do with Google Chrome), you'll find that you can clip, tag, title, and describe your web notes easily with each of the Evernote clippers.

EVERNOTE CLEARLY FOR GOOGLE CHROME

As I was writing this book, Evernote added a new extension to the mix that enables you to make your notetaking easier than ever. Evernote Clearly is a new tool that reduces all the "clutter" on your web page so that you can easily clip only the content you really want to keep. Clearly enables you to click once and hide all the extraneous items on the page—such as banner ads, navigation links, and more—so that you can focus (clearly) on what you want to grab. When you're finished reviewing the clear page, click the return arrow and Clearly returns your web page to normal display.

As of this writing, Evernote Clearly is available only for Google Chrome, but support for additional browsers might be forthcoming. Find out more about Evernote Clearly (and download it) by going to www.evernote.com/about/download/clearly.php.

Downloading and Installing the Sa' Clipper

Safari is the most pop
browser on the Mac,
available for the PC
Mac OS X Lion an'
or later, you can
the Evernote W
your machine
browser to t'
(www.evernote.com.,
and click Evernote.

1. On the Evernote page, point to the Get the Web Clipper button.

2. Drag the button to the Safari toolbar at the top of the browser window. Release the mouse button.

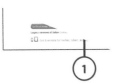

(1)

3. Type a name for the Web Clipper as you want it to appear in the toolbar.

4. Click OK.

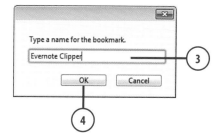

Wait—I Already Have the Clipper!

 If you are using Safari 5.0 or earlier, chances are that Evernote installed the Web Clipper automatically when you installed Evernote for OS X.

Capturing Notes on the Web

Now that you've installed the Web Clipper, you're ready for the easy part: clipping the content you want and adding it to your Evernote notes. Whether you're using Internet Explorer, Firefox, Google Chrome, or Safari, when you clip information online, a pop-up dialog box enables you to choose the selected notebook, add tags, and insert additional notes along with the clipping. What's more, Evernote keeps track of the website URL so that you never have to wonder where you got that note.

What Web Content Will You Add to Evernote?

When you're adding web clippings to Evernote, you have two choices: You can select the content on the page you want to add to your note, or you can decide to add the whole page to your Evernote note.

>> Go Further

EVERNOTE CLEARLY FOR GOOGLE CHROME

As I was writing this book, Evernote added a new extension to the mix that enables you to make your notetaking easier than ever. Evernote Clearly is a new tool that reduces all the "clutter" on your web page so that you can easily clip only the content you really want to keep. Clearly enables you to click once and hide all the extraneous items on the page—such as banner ads, navigation links, and more—so that you can focus (clearly) on what you want to grab. When you're finished reviewing the clear page, click the return arrow and Clearly returns your web page to normal display.

As of this writing, Evernote Clearly is available only for Google Chrome, but support for additional browsers might be forthcoming. Find out more about Evernote Clearly (and download it) by going to www.evernote.com/about/download/clearly.php.

Downloading and Installing the Safari Web Clipper

Safari is the most popular web browser on the Mac, but it is also available for the PC. If you're using Mac OS X Lion and running Safari 5.1 or later, you can download and install the Evernote Web Clipper to work on your machine. Start by pointing your browser to the Evernote home page (www.evernote.com), click Products, and click Evernote.

1. On the Evernote page, point to the Get the Web Clipper button.

2. Drag the button to the Safari toolbar at the top of the browser window. Release the mouse button.

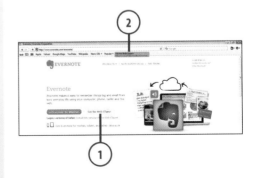

3. Type a name for the Web Clipper
   as you want it to appear in the
   toolbar.

4. Click OK.

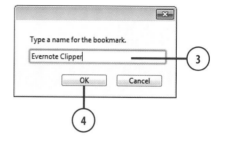

Wait—I Already Have the Clipper!

If you are using Safari 5.0 or earlier, chances are that Evernote installed the Web Clipper automatically when you installed Evernote for OS X.

Capturing Notes on the Web

Now that you've installed the Web Clipper, you're ready for the easy part: clipping the content you want and adding it to your Evernote notes. Whether you're using Internet Explorer, Firefox, Google Chrome, or Safari, when you clip information online, a pop-up dialog box enables you to choose the selected notebook, add tags, and insert additional notes along with the clipping. What's more, Evernote keeps track of the website URL so that you never have to wonder where you got that note.

What Web Content Will You Add to Evernote?

When you're adding web clippings to Evernote, you have two choices: You can select the content on the page you want to add to your note, or you can decide to add the whole page to your Evernote note.

Adding an IE Web Clipping to Evernote

⊞ If you're using Evernote on a Windows computer, your Web Clipper installs automatically, and you can activate it at any time by right-clicking the web content you want to capture.

1. Right-click anywhere on the page you want to add to your notes.

2. Click Add to Evernote 4.0. The New Clip – Evernote dialog box appears.

3. Click in the Title box and type a title for the note.

4. Click in the Tags box and type a tag and then press Tab.

5. Click the Notebook arrow and choose the name of the notebook in which you want to save the content.

6. Click Add Note.

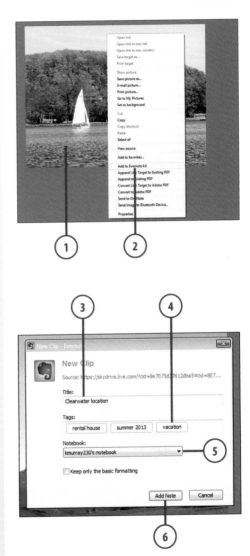

No Notebooks Yet

If you haven't created any notebooks yet, don't worry; you can leave this setting as the default and organize the notes into notebooks later if you choose. You learn more about creating and organizing your notebooks in Chapter 9, "Creating and Managing Notebooks."

Just the Facts, Ma'am

If you would rather strip out all the fancy formatting, columns, logos, and more and just add the basic text and simple format to your note page, click the Keep Only the Basic Formatting checkbox before you click Add Note.

It's Not All Good

Funky Web Content

Depending on the format of the web page and the type of content you're clipping, the note that comes into your Evernote page may be an awful mess. If this is the case, you can delete the note (simply right-click it and choose Delete Note) and go back to the web page and try again, this time clicking Keep Only the Basic Formatting checkbox.

If checking the checkbox doesn't help much, try selecting just the content you have to have before you right-click and choose Add to Evernote 4.0. By selecting only specific content, you reduce the number of extraneous features Evernote will grab by default.

Clipping Web Content in Safari

When you are browsing the web using your Safari browser, you can easily grab the content you want using the Web Clipper in the Safari toolbar. You can grab an entire page, selected content, or even make a PDF of the page (read on for more about that).

1. When you find web content you want to clip, click the Evernote Clipper tool in the Safari toolbar.

2. If you are not logged in, Evernote displays the Sign In window. Type your username.

3. Click in the Password box and type your password.

4. If you want Evernote to remember your information, click Remember Me for a Week.

5. Click Sign In.

6. The page title is displayed in the Title box, but you can click in the box and change the title if you like.

7. Click in the Tags box and type any tags you want to assign to the note.

8. Click the Notebook down-arrow and choose the notebook you want to use to save the note.

9. Click in the Add Text area and type any additional notes you want to include with the web content.

10. Click Done to add the note to your Evernote note page.

Safari Clipper for the Mac

If you're using the new Safari extension for the Mac, you can click the elephant icon to begin the process of note-taking. You can also view a collection of your recent notes by clicking the All Notes button in the Clipper pane.

Clipping Options

If you select a portion of web content before you click the Clipper tool in the toolbar, the Quicknote dialog box that opens will give you the additional options of Saving Page URL or Clip Full Page. If you want to save the web address with the small clip you've highlighted, click the Save Page URL checkbox. If you change your mind about the selection and want to clip the entire web page after all, click the Clip Full Page checkbox before clicking Save to clip the note.

Clipping Firefox Content

The process for clipping content in Firefox is similar to the steps you follow in the Safari version of the Web Clipper. You start by pointing Firefox to a web page with content you want to capture; then click the Clipper tool, add your info, and you're good to go.

1. Display the page with the content you want to clip.

2. Click the Evernote Clipper icon.

3. Click in the Title box and type a title for the note.

4. Click in the Tags box and type the tags you want to add to the note.

5. Click the Notebook arrow and choose the notebook in which you want to save the note.

6. Click Add Note.

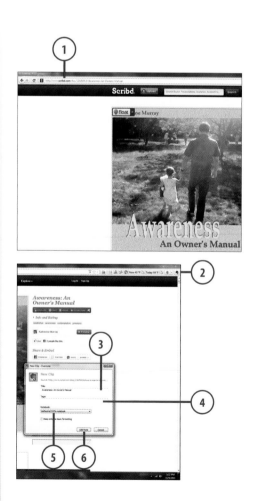

Ditto the Chrome

The process of adding a note in Google Chrome is almost identical to what you'll find in Firefox. Simply open the browser, find the web page you want to capture, and click the Evernote Clipper icon in the far-right end of the toolbar. Enter the title, tags, and text you want to keep with the note, choose your notebook of choice, and save the note. Simple, eh?

Snapping a Webcam Note

Another way you can add content to your notes pages involves grabbing an image with your webcam and plunking it on the page. This can be helpful when you need to show and tell something in your Evernote notebooks.

You can use a standard webcam to take the images, or you can use a built-in webcam on your netbook, tablet, or iPad.

>>> Go Further

HOW WILL YOU USE WEBCAM NOTES?

Before you get too excited—the webcam notes you can add in Evernote aren't *video*. Instead, they are snapshots you take on your Windows or Mac computer of whatever happens to be in front of the camera at the time. In some cases, this might be you, but in others, it might be something you simply want to capture to show on your note page. Here are a few examples:

- Have everyone on your team take a webcam photo to include in the notebook so you can all see images of your team mates.

- Hold up your design of a book cover and take a webcam picture.

- Show off your new puppy.

- Lift up the finished product for a recipe you're writing up.

- Display an org chart you've been slaving over.

Capturing a Webcam Note

Evernote includes another type of note called a Webcam Note that opens up a webcam window so that you can grab an image in real time and add it to your note. On the Mac, these types of notes are known as iSight Notes. You'll find information about adding an iSight Note to your notes in Chapter 5, "Adding and Working with Images."

1. In the Evernote window, click New Note.

2. Click New Webcam Note. The New Webcam Note window appears, with a live webcam feed.

3. Pose or smile or hold up the object you want to capture in the note.

4. Click the Take Snapshot button. After you take the snapshot, Evernote gives you the option of recapturing it.

5. If you want to recapture the image, click Retake Snapshot.

6. If you want to add the image to your note page, click Save to Evernote.

Editing Web Snapshots

You can edit an image you capture on your webcam as you would any image in your Evernote notes. Right-click the image, point to Open With, and choose the name of the program you want to use to edit the image. Additionally, you can choose Save As and save the image as a file you can then use or edit in other programs.

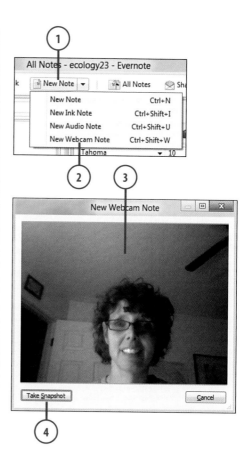

Editing Your Webcam Note

After you add the webcam snapshot to your note, you can edit it normally, adding a title, tags, and note text, formatting the text in the way you want.

It's Not All Good

No Resizing for the Webcam

Unfortunately, no easy way exists to resize the photo you add using the webcam. It is added to the note at full size, and if you want to make it smaller, you can't simply click a corner and drag it in the direction you want to resize the image. Instead, you need to right-click the image, point to Open With, and choose one of the image editors on your computer that will enable you to resize the image. After you resize the image, you can save it and close the utility, and the webcam image will be resized in your Evernote note.

Record audio notes easily in Evernote
for Windows and Evernote for Mac

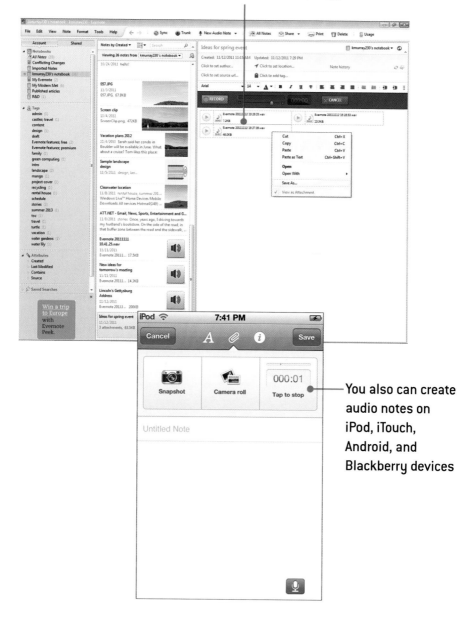

You also can create
audio notes on
iPod, iTouch,
Android, and
Blackberry devices

Do you love to hear yourself thinking out loud? If so, capture those audio clips as notes you can save in your Evernote notebook. In this chapter, you find out how to record audio notes by completing the following tasks:

8

→ Preparing to Record an Audio Note
→ Recording Your Note
→ Managing Audio Notes

Recording Audio Notes

Nobody says you have to be a note-typer or a web clipper to use Evernote effectively. In fact, many of us think best on our feet, brainstorming out loud or recording conversations we've had as a group. Evernote provides audio notes for just this purpose. You can easily add audio notes to your note pages, save them out as files you use in other formats, or even export the note so that you can gather up the audio clips and use them in other applications. This chapter shows you how to capture audio notes and work with the files you create so that you always have access to your latest and greatest ideas.

What Do You Need to Record Audio Notes?

At its most basic level, all you need to record notes in Evernote is a computer capable of recording and playing back sound. If you're using a desktop computer, this means you'll be using a microphone and speakers or a headset that includes a microphone.

When it comes to playing back the sound you record, Evernote doesn't include its own audio player as part of the program, which means you need to have a third-party app installed that *does* play sound. Luckily, all your computers and devices—Windows, Mac, and various mobile devices and phones—should all have the capacity to play sound. What's more, you likely have other apps that do the trick, too, such as Windows Media Player and Sound Recorder, for Windows.

Setting Up Your Speakers

The most thorough way on a Windows PC to make sure you have your sound equipment ready to record and play back audio is to go to the Control Panel and check out the Hardware and Sound category.

1. Click Start.

2. Click Control Panel.

3. Click Hardware and Sound.

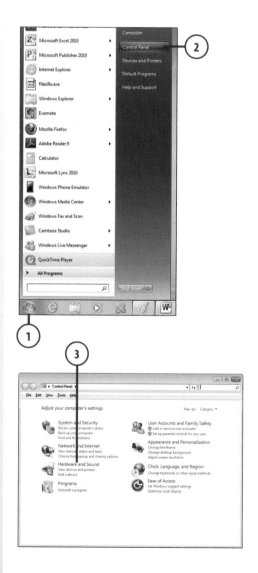

4. Click Sound. The Sound dialog box appears, offering you options you need for controlling audio playback and recording.

The Fast Route

In Windows 7, you can also type Sound in the Start menu's Search field and then select the Sound applet in the results that appear.

5. Click the item that is set as the Default Device.

6. Click Properties. The Speakers Properties dialog box appears.

7. Click the Levels tab.

8. Make sure the speakers are set to play sound, and adjust the Speakers volume slider to the level you want.

9. Click OK.

Adjusting Volume Easily

When you know that sound is playing correctly on your computer, you can use the volume control buttons on your Windows or Mac keyboard—or the Volume icon in the system tray of your Windows desktop—to increase or decrease the volume.

What Kinds of Sound Files Play in Evernote?

The types of sound files you can play in Evernote will depend on the types of players you have installed on your computer because Evernote doesn't include its own media player. This means that if you're using a Windows machine, you can use any file that can play in Windows Media Player; if you're using a Mac, anything that runs in QuickTime can be played. You can also add any type of file to a note as an attachment—for example, you can attach an .aac or .mp4 file, but you'll only be able to play it back if you have a player on your system that supports that file format.

Setting Microphone Levels

You can also adjust your microphone levels—both to check the mic is working properly and to set the volume control so you're recording at a level loud enough for you to hear later.

1. In the Sound dialog box, click the Recording tab.

2. Click the Default Device.

3. Click Properties. The Microphone Properties dialog box opens.

4. Click the Levels tab.

5. Adjust the Microphone slider to set the sound sensitivity level of your microphone.

6. Adjust the Microsoft Boost setting to indicate how much you want the sound enhanced (over background noise) as you record.

7. Click OK twice to close both dialog boxes.

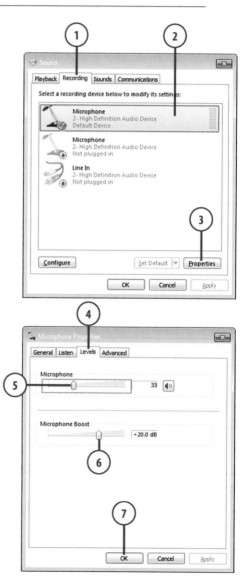

THINKING THROUGH SPACE CONSIDERATIONS

Depending on how much you're recording when you capture audio notes and how often you record them, you may need to think through how you capture notes so that you can optimize the amount of space you have available in your free Evernote account. As you know, Evernote limits your usage to 60MB per month. If you upgrade to a premium account, your usage limit for monthly notes is increased to 1GB—considerably more!

To give you an idea of how much space your audio notes might require, consider this. By way of example, I created an audio note of myself reading the Gettysburg Address, a task that took two minutes of recorded time. The file size of the audio note is 200KB. Because each megabyte (MB) contains 1,024 kilobytes (KB), that means I could record approximately 300 audio notes of the same size before I would max out the 60MB usage.

For the premium account, Evernote estimates that you can create and store 450 audio notes per month, but if you're a free user, always keep an eye on the size and number of audio notes you create.

Recording Your Note

The process of adding an audio note in Evernote requires just a few simple steps. You start a new note, click Record, speak your piece, and click Stop. The audio note is then added to the note and you can play it back whenever you like by clicking play. When your notes are synchronized with your web Evernote account, the audio note will be available online as well.

Audio Notes on Your Desktop

When you know your microphone and speakers are working properly, you can record your note easily by starting a new audio note.

1. In Evernote, click the New Ink Note arrow at the top of the Evernote window.

2. Click New Audio Note.

3. Click in the title area and type a title for your note.

4. Click Record. The Record buttons turns into a Save button, and you can begin speaking into your microphone. Evernote records everything you say.

5. Click Save. The saved note appears in the note window, telling you the name of the audio sound click (which will look something like Evernote 20111112 19.29.23.wav) and the size of the file.

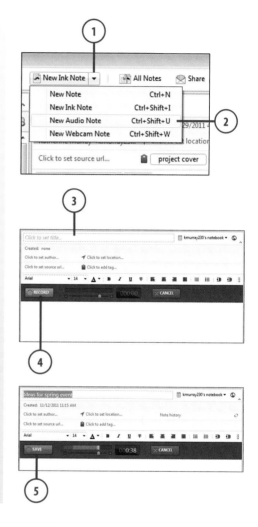

Start an Audio Note the Easy Way

You can also use a shortcut key to start a new audio note on your Windows PC: Press Ctrl+Shift+U to get started.

Recording Multiple Notes

You can add more than one audio note to a note in Evernote. If you click Record and record multiple note segments, Evernote places all the clips in the same note, with the most recent audio clip listed in the top right of the note window.

Recording Mac Notes

When you want to record an audio note on your Mac system, display the Evernote window and click Audio Note in the top center of the Evernote window. Record the note and click Save to add the clip to the new note.

Audio Notes on Your Mobile Device

Evernote also supports audio notes on various phone and mobile devices. For example, you can add voice notes on the iPhone, iPod touch, and iPad, as well as Android and Blackberry devices. The following process describes the process for recording an audio note on an iPod touch. Begin by launching Evernote, and tap the + to start a new note.

1. Tap the microphone icon (labeled Audio) to begin recording. A small red microphone appears in the lower-right corner, letting you know that recording is in process.

2. After you're done recording, tap the timer in the upper-right area of the screen to stop the recording.

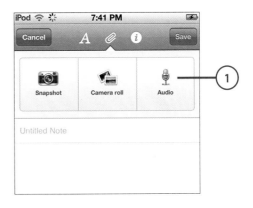

3. The audio file is added to the note. You can listen to it if you like by tapping View Attachments.

4. If you want to re-record the note, tap Audio again. This replaces the original recording you captured.

5. Tap Untitled Audio Note to add a title to the new note.

6. Tap Save to save the audio note to Evernote.

Adding Android Audio

If you want to record an audio note on your Android device, start Evernote and tap New Note. Tap the microphone icon that appears on the toolbar, and record your note. Tap the Stop button to attach the clip to your note.

Recording Interruptions

If you are recording on your Android device and find that the recording stops as soon as you go to switch apps, be sure that you're pressing and holding the Home key rather than just tapping it. Tapping the Home key closes open apps and takes you back to the Home screen; but pressing and holding the Home key enables you to switch among open applications.

>>> Go Further

RECORDING AUDIO NOTES ON YOUR WINDOWS PHONE 7

When you want to record an audio note on your Windows Phone 7, launch Evernote and tap + to start a new note. In the new note window, tap and then type a title for the note, and then tap the Record tool in the bottom right of the tools row at the bottom of the note window.

On the Recording screen that appears, speak your note into your phone. The sound gauge shows the volume Evernote is recording. When you've finished speaking, tap Stop. The note is added to the current note. You can play the note by tapping it and then tapping Play. If you want to delete the note and record again, tap Delete and then, in the note window, tap the Record tool again to re-record.

Managing Your Audio Notes

After Evernote adds the audio note to your notes, you can play it back whenever you like by clicking the play button. After Evernote syncs your notebooks, you'll also be able to listen to your note from any device or browser. In addition, you can save the sound clip as a file so that you can use it in other programs in addition to Evernote.

Installing a Playback Plug-In

When you view your Evernote notebook on the web, you may need to download a plug-in before the audio note will play correctly. Chances are you won't need this plug-in with Internet Explorer, but with Firefox and Google Chrome you might.

1. Display your Evernote notes online, logging in if necessary.

2. Click the note that includes the audio you want to listen to.

3. Click Install Missing Plugins. The Plugin Finder Service dialog box appears.

4. Select the plugin you want to add. If the plugin is not found, click Manual Install. The Apple QuickTime page is displayed.

5. Click Next.

6. Click the Download Now button.

7. In the Opening QuickTimeInstaller.exe dialog box, click Save File. The Downloads dialog box appears and the installer begins downloading.

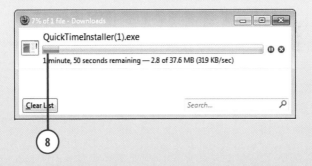

8. After the installer downloads, double-click the filename to install Quick Time.

9. Finally, back in the Plugin Finder Service dialog box, click Finish to complete the process. Now when you return to Evernote in your web browser, you will be able to see and play the audio in your note.

SENDING NOTES WITH SIRI

Go Further

If you've set up your iPhone to send notes to Evernote via email, you can use Siri, the new iPhone 4S digital assistant, to send notes directly to your Evernote account. To try it, simply launch Siri on your phone and say, "Send email to Evernote." You can then speak the content of your message and say "Send." If you want to send a short, sweet note, you can say something like "Send email to Evernote. Remember to print handouts for tomorrow's meeting. Send." The entire note will go to your Evernote account with no further action from you. Nice.

Saving Your Audio Clips

Although having your audio notes tucked safely away in Evernote is great, sometimes you might like to include those audio notes in other projects. For example, you might want to add a note you recorded to a presentation in PowerPoint, or perhaps you want to add a little welcome message to your online store.

1. In Evernote, display the audio note with the clip you want to save.

2. Right-click the clip. A context menu of options appears.

3. Click Save As. The Save As dialog box appears.

4. Navigate to the folder in which you want to save the file.

5. Enter a new name for the file if you want (but leave the .wav extension at the end of the filename).

6. Click Save.

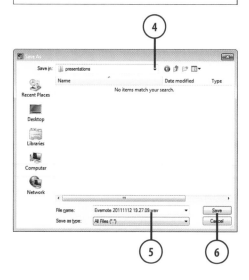

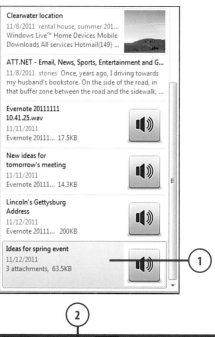

EXPORTING YOUR AUDIO CLIPS

No specific feature enables you to export only your audio notes, but you can explore your notes and retrieve the audio files by exporting the notes as HTML and then locating the audio files.

Begin by selecting the notes you want to explore. Click File to open the File menu, click Export, and choose Export As a Single HTML Web Page (.html). Click Export.

In the Save As dialog box, choose the folder where you want to save the exported HTML files and click Save. Evernote exports the notes you selected. Click the Open Containing Folder button in the Export Succeeded dialog box. Click the Evernote.enex_files folder to see the files (images and audio clips) that are included in the notes you exported, and copy and move the .wav files to the location where you want to save and work with the audio files.

Creating a new notebook is a simple task on both Windows and Mac computers

You can create up to 250 synchronized notebooks in Evernote

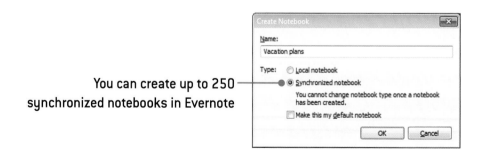

You can easily create, manage, and organize multiple notebooks in Evernote to keep all your interests straight. In this chapter, you learn to create and manage notebooks in Evernote by learning the following tasks:

→ Creating a New Notebook
→ Managing Notebooks
→ Working with Notebook Stacks
→ Importing Notebooks

Creating and Managing Notebooks

Evernote makes it easy for you to add all kinds of notes and add tags so that you can find your notes again later. But if you're working on a specific project or want to organize your notes into specific groups so that you can find information, notebooks are the way to go. You can easily create, manage, and share your notebooks in Evernote, and that's what this chapter is all about.

Creating a New Notebook

Creating a new notebook is a simple task in Evernote. You can create two types of notebooks. *Synchronized* notebooks are notebooks that sync automatically to your Evernote account online as well as your other computers and devices running Evernote, so all your notebooks include the latest notes. You can also create *local* notebooks, which remain on the computer where you create them. Local notebooks aren't synchronized with your notebooks online—instead, they stay securely on your computer, which makes local notebooks ideal for the information you want to keep close to home.

Notebooks on Mobile Devices

Evernote makes accessing and updating your notes and notebooks on your mobile device easy, but depending on the type of mobile device you use, you might not be able to create new notebooks or change notebook properties. As of this writing, only Android phones can create new notebooks (simply tap the Menu button and tap New Notebook).

How Many Notebooks Do You Want?

Notebooks give you a handy way to organize notes in categories you can access and work with easily. You can also organize your notebooks into groups called *stacks* to help you keep like information together. Evernote has a maximum limit of 250 notebooks so if you're thinking of putting a library-sized note collection on Evernote that would require an enormous number of notebooks, think through how you want to use your notebooks before you begin creating them.

Creating a Synchronized Notebook

By default, the notebooks you create in Evernote are synchronized notebooks. This means that the notebooks sync automatically to your Evernote account online, and then, by extension, they update to the Evernote accounts you have on other computers and devices as well, when you log in to Evernote. This helps you keep all your notes synchronized across multiple computers and devices.

1. In the Evernote window, click File. The File menu opens.

2. Click New Notebook. The Create Notebook dialog box appears.

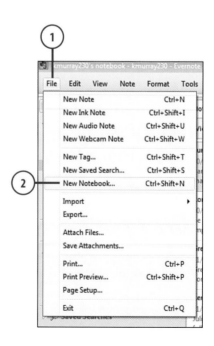

3. Type a name for the notebook in the Name box.

4. Leave Synchronized Notebook selected.

5. Click the option to make this new notebook the default notebook.

6. Click OK. The new notebook is added.

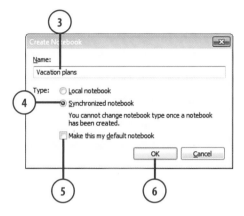

WHAT ARE YOUR EVERNOTE LIMITS?

>> Go Further

Evernote has a generous spirit with regard to the number of notes, notebooks, tags, and searches you can create. Here's a quick run-down:

- You can create 100,000 notes!

- Each note can be up to 25MB if you have a free account, or 50MB if you have a premium account.

- You can create up to 250 synchronized notebooks.

- You can create an unlimited number of local notebooks.

- You can create and add up to 10,000 tags to your Evernote notes.

- You can create 100 saved searches for note topics you want to find regularly.

Creating a Local Notebook

When you create a new notebook in Evernote, you are given the choice of creating a synchronized or local notebook. Synchronized is selected by default. Create a local notebook for any notebook you want to keep on your computer without synchronizing it to your Evernote account online or your notebooks on other computers and devices. You might want to use a local notebook, for example, to store sensitive financial information, your kids' medical records, or other data that you want to make sure is for your eyes only.

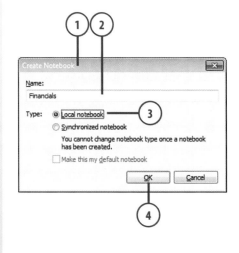

1. Press Ctrl+Shift+N to display the Create Notebook dialog box.

2. Type in a name for the notebook.

3. Click Local Notebook.

4. Click OK.

You're Stuck with Your Notebook Type

When you make the choice about what kind of notebook you want to create, be sure to consider your options carefully because after you make the call, you're stuck with it. You can't change the type from Synchronized to Local or vice versa after you've created the notebook. At that point your only recourse is to create a new notebook with the style you want and move all the notes to the new notebook with the correct style. (You'll learn how to do that later in this chapter.)

Changing Defaults Later

You might use one notebook as your default for awhile, and then when you move on to a new project or begin working with a different team, you might want to change your default notebook. You can do this on a Windows computer by right-clicking the notebook you want to make the default, clicking Properties, and clicking the Make This My Default Notebook checkbox. On a Mac, press and hold ⌘ and click the notebook you want to use; then click Notebook Settings and click to check the Make This My Default Notebook. Click OK to close the dialog box.

Managing Your Notebooks

When you add notebooks to Evernote, they appear in the Notebooks area at the top of the left panel in the Evernote window. You can simply move from one note to another by clicking the notebook you want to see. You might want to rename or delete a notebook, or perhaps move or copy notes from one notebook to another.

Renaming a Notebook

You might find from time to time that you want to rename a notebook you're using. Perhaps the name of a project has changed, or you want to change the name so that others can easily find it. Whatever your reason, you can change the name of a notebook and Evernote will synchronize the change automatically (if the notebook in question is a synchronized notebook).

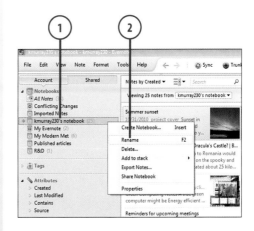

1. In the notebook list, right-click the name of the notebook you want to rename.

2. Click Rename.

3. Type a new name for the note-book.

4. Click outside the notebook name to save your change.

Undoing Renames

You can't undo your change by pressing Ctrl+Z or choosing Undo from the Edit menu after you've renamed a notebook. If you aren't happy with the change, follow the preceding steps again.

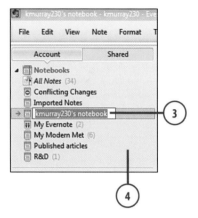

Copying Notes to Other Notebooks

You can copy a note and paste it into the notebook you select. Here's a quirky thing, however; for some reason Evernote doesn't give you the means to copy multiple notes, so you have to copy selected notes one at a time. You can copy notes by using the Copy command in the Note menu or you can right-click the note you want to copy and choose Copy from the list that appears.

1. Right-click the note you want to copy.

2. Point to Copy Note. A pop-up list appears.

3. Click Notebook. The Copy Note to Notebook dialog box appears.

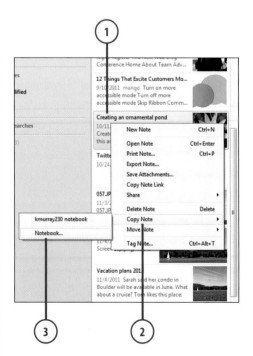

4. Scroll down the list until you see the notebook you want to copy the note to.

5. Click the notebook in the list.

6. Click Preserve Created and Updated Dates if you want to keep information about the dates the note was created and updated.

7. Click Preserve Tags if you want to preserve the tags assigned to the note.

8. Click Copy.

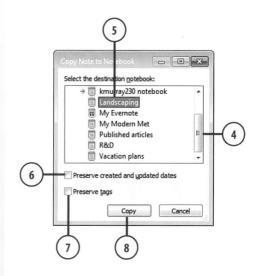

Managing Notebooks on Windows and Mac Computers

All the tasks involved in managing your notebooks—renaming them, moving notes, copying notes, and deleting notebooks—work the same whether you're using a Windows computer or a Macintosh. To right-click on your Mac, press Ctrl while you click the mouse button.

Moving Notes to a Different Notebook

Organizing and reorganizing your notes means that you may regularly move notes from notebook to notebook—especially if you create shared notebooks with select information you want everyone on your team to be able to view. You can easily move notes from one notebook to another in Evernote.

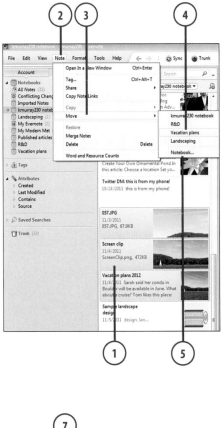

1. Select all notes you want to move to the new notebook.

2. Click Note to open the Note menu.

3. Point to Move.

4. In the pop-up menu that appears, click the name of the notebook to which you want to move the notes.

5. If you don't see the notebook in the list, click Notebook.

6. In the Move Note to Notebook dialog box, scroll to display the notebook you need.

7. Click the notebook.

8. Click Move. The notes are moved to the new location.

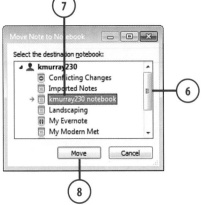

Selecting Multiple Notes

If you want to choose more than one note to move to another notebook, click the first note and then press and hold Ctrl while clicking additional notes.

Deleting Notebooks

After your need for a notebook has run its course, you can delete it using the Delete Notebook command in Evernote. Deleting unnecessary notebooks is a good idea—first, because it frees up unused free space in your usage allotment, and second, because it lessens the number of notebooks you have (250 is the limit for the number of notebooks you can create in Evernote).

1. Right-click the notebook you want to delete.

2. In the menu that appears, click Delete. The Confirm Action dialog box appears.

3. Click Delete Notebook and the notebook—and any notes it contains—is removed from Evernote.

You Can't Delete Notebooks the Mobile Way

If you are using Evernote on your mobile device, you'll need to wait to delete a notebook until you're using either the desktop version of Evernote or the web version.

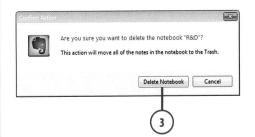

Go Further

A FEW MORE LIMITS ON DELETING

Evernote is easygoing with regard to deleting the notebooks you've created, with a couple small exceptions. You won't be able to delete the only remaining notebook in your Evernote account, and you won't be able to remove the All Notes notebook displayed in the notebooks area in the top-left panel of the Evernote window.

Exporting Notebooks

You might have some situations in which you want to export notes from one notebook so that you can import them in another notebook on a different machine. You might do this, for example, if you are using a local notebook and don't want to sync it to the web or share it with other users.

1. Right-click the notebook you want to export.

2. In the menu that appears, click Export Notes.

3. In the Export dialog box, choose the format you want to use for the exported file.

4. Click Export.

Choosing an Export Format

You can choose different formats for the exported file, depending on what you plan to do with it. If you plan to import the file to another Evernote notebook at some point, export the notes in the .enex format. If you would rather be able to read the notes in their exported format, choose the .html format.

EXPORTING NOTE ATTRIBUTES

As you know, you can assign all sorts of attributes to your Evernote notes. If you plan to import your notes back to an Evernote notebook later, you might want to have Evernote export all the attributes you've assigned to the notes as well. To have Evernote export the attributes, click the Options button in the Export dialog box.

A list of seven attributes—Note title, Created date, Updated date, Author, Location, Tags, and Source URL—appears so that you can click the checkboxes of the attributes you want to include. Click OK to save your selection, and then click Export in the dialog box to complete the operation.

Importing Notebooks

Evernote enables you to export your notebooks so that you can use the information in other places and in other ways. You can also import exported notebooks—both from Evernote and from Microsoft OneNote—so you always have access to the notes you need.

Importing Evernote Notebooks

When you import an exported file from your Evernote notebook, the file opens and the notes are available in your Evernote notebook just as they were before they were exported.

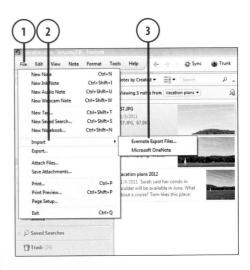

1. Click File to open the File menu.

2. Point to Import. A pop-up list appears.

3. Click Evernote Export Files on Evernote for Windows. If you're using Evernote for Mac, click Import from Archive.

4. In the Open dialog box, navigate to the folder containing the Evernote export file.

5. Click the file.

6. Leave the Import Note Tags checkbox selected if you want to import tags.

7. Click Open.

8. Evernote tells you that the data was imported and gives you the name of the notebook. Click Yes to place the data in the notebook.

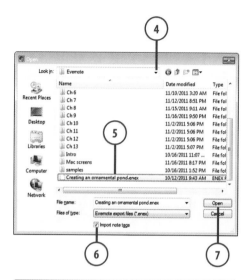

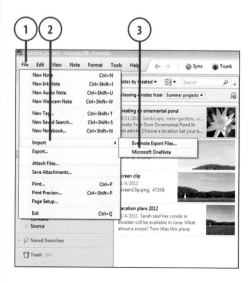

Importing OneNote Notebooks

If you've been using Microsoft OneNote, you'll be happy to know you can import notebooks directly into your Evernote account.

1. Click File to open the File menu.

2. Point to Import.

3. This time, point to Microsoft OneNote.

4. In the OneNote Import dialog box, click the arrow to choose the notebook you want to import from the list that appears.

5. Click the checkboxes for the sections you want to import in the selected notebook.

6. Click OK. Evernote imports the notes from the OneNote folder and displays a message box telling you where the imported notes will be stored.

7. Click Yes to complete the operation.

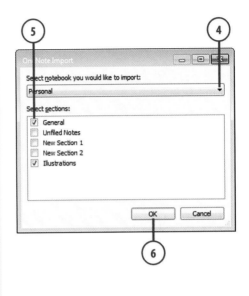

Now They Are Evernote Notes

After your OneNote notes are imported into your Evernote notebooks, they appear in the Evernote screen just like any other Evernote note. Now you can add tags and all the different note attributes you normally would add to a note, and Evernote will synchronize the new notes with your web account and with other notebooks when you log in using other computers or mobile devices.

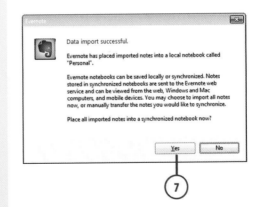

Working with Notebook Stacks

Similar to the way in which you can group similar notes into notebooks, you can put together groups of notebooks in what Evernote calls *stacks*. This enables you to easily group notebooks that belong together. For example, if you use Evernote to manage your small business, you might create a stack of notebooks that are all related to various business tasks—Financials, Ordering, Inventory, New Products, and so on. You can create a notebook stack by choosing a command from the context menu, or you can create one by dragging and dropping a notebook in the notebooks area. This section introduces you to both methods.

Creating and Naming a Notebook Stack

Creating a notebook stack is as simple as right-clicking a notebook and choosing the command to add a new stack to your note book list.

1. Right-click the notebook you want to add to a stack.

2. In the menu that appears, point to Add to Stack.

3. Click New Stack. The selected notebook is placed in the new stack, and the name Notebook Stack is displayed at the top of the list entry.

4. Right-click the new Notebook Stack.

5. Click Rename.

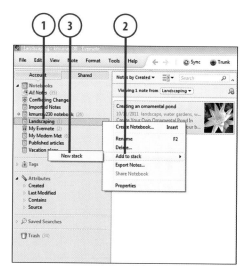

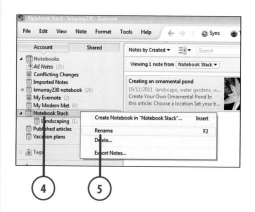

6. Type the new name for the note-book stack.

7. Click outside the stack title to save the change.

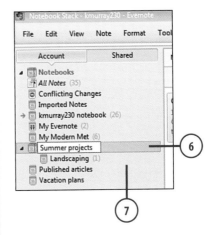

Adding Notebooks to a Stack

When you add a notebook to an existing stack, you can do it two ways: by right-clicking the notebook and adding it to the stack displayed in the stack list, or by dragging the notebook in the notebook list to the stack you want in which you want it to appear.

1. Right-click the notebook you want to add to a stack.

2. Point to Add to Stack.

3. Click the name of the stack in the list to which you want to add the notebook. The notebook appears in the stack you selected.

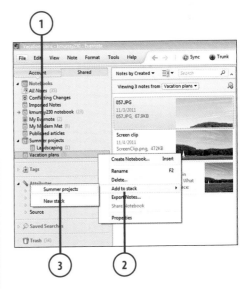

Moving Notebooks Among the Stacks
Reorganizing your notebooks is a simple matter of dragging and dropping notebooks from one stack to another. You can move notebooks as many times as you like.

Stacks Are Notebooks?
Remember Evernote's limits? For some reason, Evernote counts each stack you create as another one of your 250 allowed notebooks in Evernote. So if you have so many note-books that you're pushing the limit set by Evernote, you may want to remove some unneeded notebooks before you add stacks in Evernote.

Enter search text to
find the notes you want

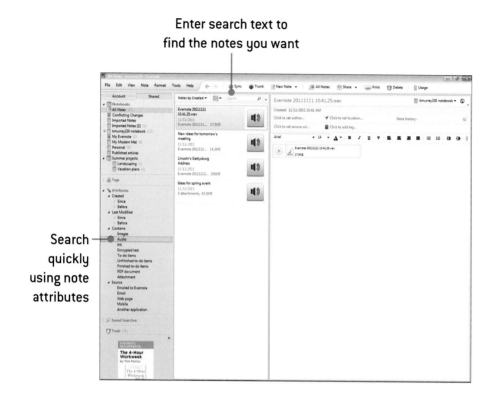

Search
quickly
using note
attributes

Choose your favorite
notes view

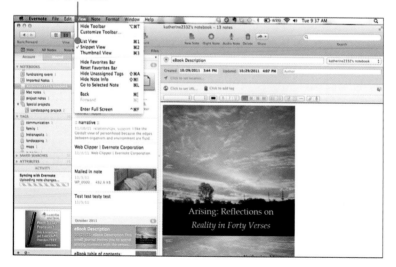

When you have created dozens—or hundreds—of notes as well as multiple notebooks, you need to be able to find the notes you need quickly. Evernote makes this fast and simple. In this chapter, you learn to find just the notes you're looking for by completing the following tasks:

→ Searching for a Note

→ Displaying Evernote Views

→ Customizing the Evernote Window

Finding and Viewing Notes Your Way

So if you've been accumulating notes for any length of time—typing new notes on your desktop computers or mobile devices, recording audio notes, grabbing pictures, sketching ink notes, and more—chances are good that you've collected quite a few pieces of information. In Chapter 9, "Creating and Managing Notebooks," you learned how to organize your growing volume of notes into notebooks and notebook stacks. In this chapter, you learn how to move quickly to that one piece of information you know you stored here—somewhere.

Evernote offers you a number of ways to find quickly the information for which you're looking. You can search on virtually any note attribute to find what you need. You can also create saved searches to help you use the same search criteria over and over again. After you find the notes you're looking for, you can choose to view them in a number of different ways.

Searching for a Note

You remember writing something about Madagascar sometime last year when you were looking at exotic locations for next year's conference. But you can't remember the name of the hotel, and you're not quite sure when you created the note. How will you find it? The most obvious thing is to search for the word *Madagascar*. If you didn't use that word specifically in the note (or maybe you misspelled it), you can search for a portion of the word—or any word you might have included in the note text. This section shows you the various ways you can search for and find the notes you seek.

Doing a Simple Search

The easiest way to search for a specific note in Evernote is to click All Notes and then click in the search box and type a word or phrase reflecting the content you want to find. You can also expand the search options and choose a specific notebook in which to search.

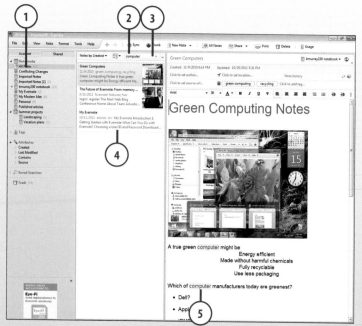

1. In the notebooks list, click All Notes.
2. Click in the search box.
3. Type a word or phrase that reflects the content you want to find.
4. Evernote lists any notes you have that contain the word *computer*.
5. The search word or phrase is highlighted wherever it appears in the currently selected note.

Fine-Tuning the Search

You can adjust the search to change the notebook you're searching or add or remove search conditions.

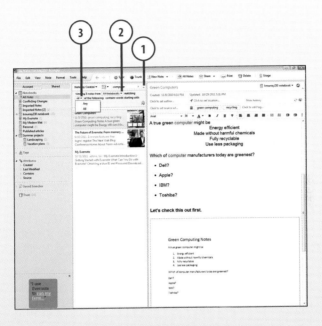

1. After your first search, click the More arrow to display additional search information.

2. Click the Notebooks arrow and choose the notebook you want to search.

3. Click the All arrow if you'd like to change the setting from All to Any. The results in the note area in the center column of the screen changes as you change the search settings. Use All when you want your search results to contain all the words you entered in your search phrase; use Any when you want to find notes that include any of the search words you entered.

Searching Within a Note

If you want to find specific content within the selected note, you can press Ctrl+F on a Windows or ⌘+F on a Mac computer. A small search box opens at the bottom of the note window, where you can type the text you want to find and click Next or Previous.

⊞ Searching with Note Attributes

Another way you can search quickly in Evernote for Windows involves search-ing for specific note attributes. Suppose, for example, that you recorded an audio note about holiday events some time ago and now you can't remem-ber which notebook you stored the note in. You can easily display only the audio notes—or only notes created after a specific date, or notes you emailed to your Evernote account, and so on.

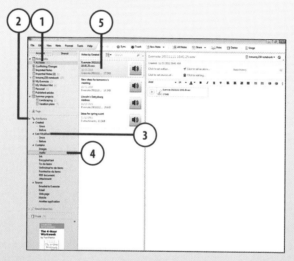

1. Click All Notes.

2. Click the Attributes arrow to display the list.

3. Click the arrow of any attributes you want to use in the search to display more specific attributes.

4. Click the attribute you want to use in the search.

5. The results appear in the notes list in the center of the Evernote window.

WHAT TYPES OF ATTRIBUTES CAN YOU SEARCH?

So which attributes can you use to narrow your search? You have plenty of options: You can search for notes that

- Were created before or after a specific date

- Were modified before or after a specific date

- Contain Evernote items (images, audio, ink, encrypted text, to-do items, PDFs, and attachments)

- Were emailed to Evernote

- Originated in an email message

- Were clipped from a web page

- Were sent from a mobile device

- Were added from another application

Creating a Saved Search

If you have a search you use regularly, you can save your search specifications so that you can apply the search at other times. Begin by choosing the search conditions or attributes you want to include in the search, and then click the Create Saved Search button.

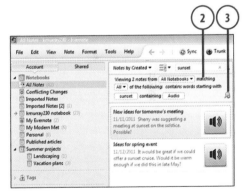

1. To the right of the search box, click the More button.

2. Set the search criteria you want to save.

3. Click the Create Saved Search to open the Create Saved Search dialog box.

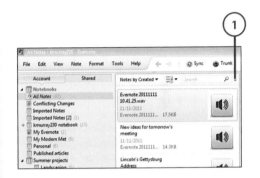

4. Type a name for the saved search in the Name field.

5. Click OK. The saved search is listed in the Saved Search area at the bottom of the panel on the left of the Evernote window.

Using a Saved Search

When you want to apply a saved search, begin by clicking the notebook you want to search (or click All Notes if you want to search all your notes) and then click the Saved Searches arrow to display the list of saved searches, and click the search you want to apply.

Displaying Evernote Views

Evernote offers a number of views you can use to display your notes in the way that make most sense to you. If you're a visual person, you might like to see the notes in thumbnail view, or if the text is what matters to you, you might want to see the whole list in snippet view. Evernote includes three different views you can use on both Windows and Mac systems: List, Snippet, and Thumbnail, with Snippet used as the default view.

List View

List view displays your notes in a three-panel format with the notebook panel on the left and the list of notes in the top-right area of the screen. Display List view by clicking View to open the View menu and clicking List View. You can also use the Windows shortcut key Ctrl+F5 to display List view.

Choose the notebook you want to view   **Click to arrange by attribute**   **Search for note information**   **Click to sort by column heading**

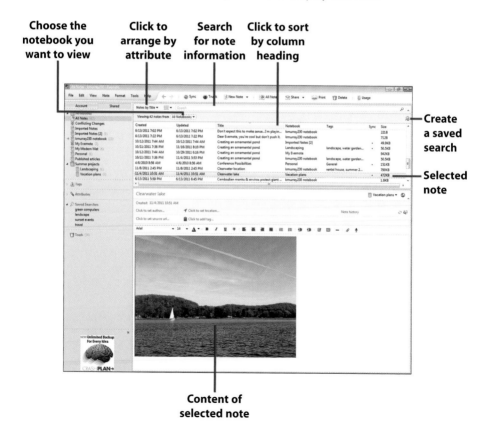

Create a saved search

Selected note

Content of selected note

Mac's List View

To display List view on the Mac, press ⌘+1. You can also display List view by clicking the List View tool at the top of the Evernote window. Snippet and Thumbnail Views tools at the top of the Evernote window display those views, respectively.

Snippet View

Snippet view displays all your notes in a panel in the center of the Evernote window. The selected note appears in the panel on the right side of the window, with the notebook panel on the left. You can use the Ctrl+F6 Windows shortcut key to display Snippet view.

Choose your notebook **Click to sort by attribute** **Search for notes** **Create a saved search**

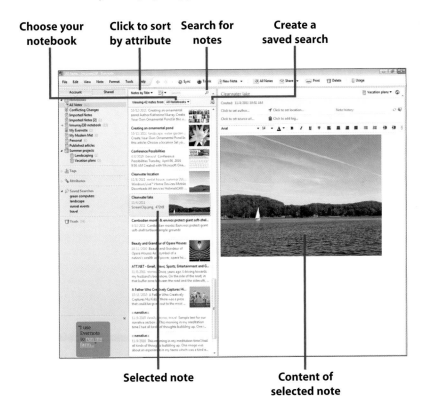

Selected note   **Content of selected note**

Snippet View on the Mac

You can display Snippet view on the Mac by pressing ⌘+2 or by clicking the Snippet View tool in the top of the Evernote window.

Thumbnail View

Thumbnail view shows the contents of all your notes in a reduced size, showing any images that are included as part of the note. You can display Thumbnail view using the Windows shortcut key Ctrl+F7.

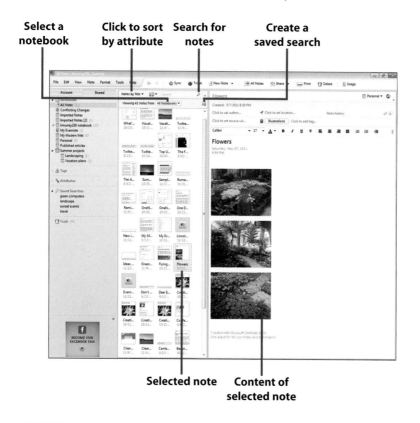

Select a notebook • Click to sort by attribute • Search for notes • Create a saved search

Selected note • Content of selected note

Displaying Thumbnail View on the Mac

To display Thumbnail view on the Mac, press ⌘+3 or click the Thumbnail View tool at the top of the Evernote window.

Customizing the Evernote Window

You can customize the Evernote window to display different configurations of panels and toolbars. You can control the display of all the panels in the Evernote window—as well as the Editing toolbar, which appears at the top of the note window, just below the attributes area.

The View menu contains all the tools you need to hide and display the various panels in the Evernote window. To change the display in Evernote for Windows, click View and choose one of the following options to toggle the display on and off:

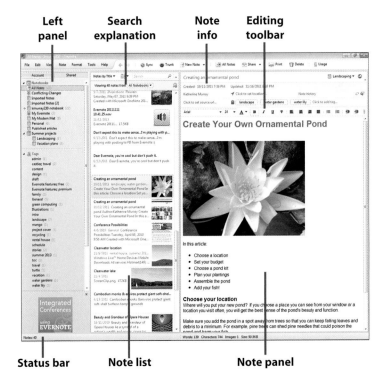

Left panel   **Search explanation**   **Note info**   **Editing toolbar**

Status bar   **Note list**   **Note panel**

If you are using Evernote for Mac, you'll find a slightly different configuration in the Mac Evernote window. You can customize the display by clicking the View menu and toggling off or on the options by clicking them.

Favorites   **Toolbar**   **Note Info**

Showing the Note History

The last tool on the View menu, Show Note History, is available only if you are a premium account user. If you have a premium account, you'll be able to view all the changes you've made previously to a note (and if the note is shared, you'll be able to see the other authors who have contributed to the note).

Use Print Preview to review your notes before you print

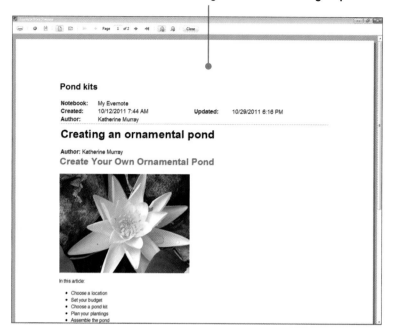

Mac Print dialog

Windows Print dialog

Storing your notes online where you can reach them easily is convenient, but sometimes you'll need to print them, too. You can easily preview and print your notes in Evernote. In this chapter, you learn how to preview and print your notes by completing the following tasks:

→ Setting Up Your Page
→ Previewing Your Note
→ Printing Notes and Notebooks

Previewing and Printing Your Notes

One of the great things about Evernote is that it makes your notes available on all the computers and devices you have access to. Not only can you display your notebooks on your Windows or Mac computer, but you can get to your Evernote account on the web anywhere you have web access, and you can continually update and review your Evernote notebooks using apps on your mobile phone.

But even though your notes are available electronically anywhere and anytime you want them, sometimes you might want to print notes from your Evernote notebooks. Perhaps you want to make a folder of all the latest notes on a particular project, or maybe you've been working on pulling together content for a report you're creating and now you're ready to print and distribute the report.

Whatever your reason for printing, you can easily choose the note pages you want to print and print the information—on your printer or to a file. This chapter shows you how to preview and print your notes and create PDF files of the notes along the way, too.

Setting Up Your Page

Most of us think of a traditional page as being an 8.5-by-11–inch sheet of paper; that's the common size used in printers and for reviewing reports and memos, but it's certainly not your only option. Evernote gives you the option of setting up your page size by choosing your paper size, the source for the paper, the page orientation (covered later in this chapter), and the margins used when printing your page.

Starting with a Saved Search

You don't have to choose a notebook when you are looking for the notes you want to print; you could click one of your saved searches or click a note attribute if that displays the notes you need in the results area. For more information about finding and viewing the notes you want, see Chapter 10, "Finding and Viewing Notes Your Way."

Choosing Paper Size and Source

The size of the paper you choose in the Page Setup dialog box depends on the type of note you want to print. Among the page sizes you can choose are a number of photo papers, index cards, and envelopes, as well as traditional and legal paper sizes. You'll find all the choices you need in the Page Setup dialog box.

1. Click File to open the File menu.

2. Click Page Setup. The settings you enter in the Page Setup dialog will apply to all your notes by default.

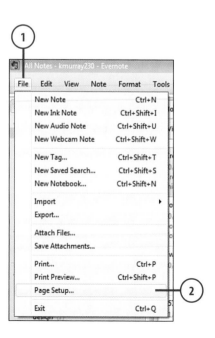

3. Click the Size arrow and select the paper size of the page on which you want to print the notes.

4. Click the Source arrow and choose the Source for the paper.

5. Click to change the orientation if you want the notes to print in Landscape instead of Portrait mode.

6. Click OK to save your settings.

Choosing a Printer Source

Depending on the type of printer you use, you might have different print trays that contain different types of paper. If this is the case, Source might include a number of different print trays, and you'll need to know which one contains the paper size you need. Click that selection in the Source list and Evernote will pull the paper from that tray when printing.

Display Page Setup Setting on the Mac

You can display the Page Setup dialog box quickly on your Mac by pressing Shift+⌘+P.

Setting Page Margins

The margins of your page control how much white space appears between the edge of the print and the sides of the page. You may want to experiment with margins a bit before you settle on the settings you like. If you plan to put the notes in a binder, you may want to make sure the inside margin is greater than the outside margin.

1. Open the Page Setup dialog box by selecting Page Setup from the File menu or by pressing Ctrl+Shift+P.

2. In the Margins area, type the new values you want to apply to the margin settings. Depending on your needs, you might have to experiment a bit to find the margins that best suit your needs

3. Click OK to save your settings and close the Page Setup dialog box.

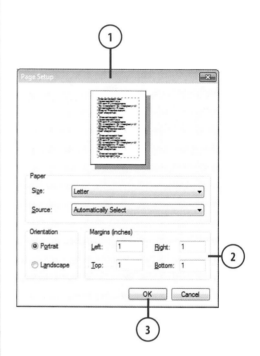

Margin Values

The settings for the margins in the Page Setup dialog box are displayed in inches. So 1 equals one inch, a standard margin for most documents. Your printer likely has its own print margin (perhaps set at .5 from the edge of the page), so even if you reduce the print margin to .25, your printer may prohibit printing beyond that .5 border of white space around the edges of the page.

Previewing Your Note

You can preview selected notes to get an idea of what the printouts will look like in printed form. You can change the orientation of the page, move through multiple pages, and zoom or reduce the display before printing. Preview can be especially helpful when you've used a number of images on your note pages; when you preview the images, you get a good sense of how they will appear on the printed page. If necessary, you can go back and reduce the size of the images or edit them before you print.

Displaying Notes in Print Preview

When you're ready to take a look at how your notes will look when they are printed, you can select the notes you want to see and preview them in Evernote. Print Preview makes it easy for you to page through your notes and make sure the notes look the way you want them to before you print.

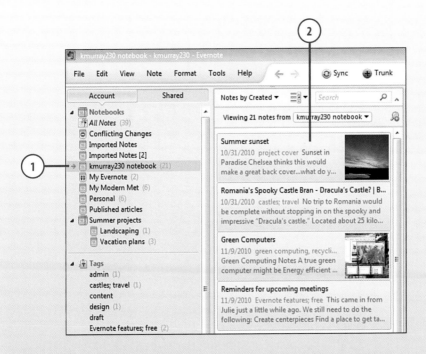

1. In Evernote, click the notebook containing the notes you want to print.

2. In the notes list, select the notes you want to print.

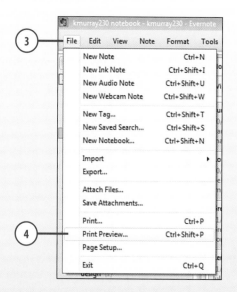

3. Click the File menu.

4. Click Print Preview.

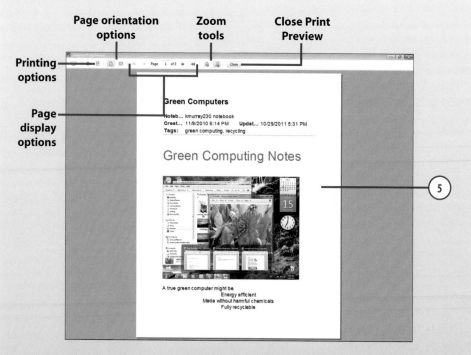

Page orientation options

Zoom tools

Close Print Preview

Printing options

Page display options

5. The Print Preview window displays the first note you had selected in the notes list. You can use the tools at the top of the Preview window to change the preview of the notes you want to print.

Previewing on the Mac

Print Preview on the Mac works a little differently. Instead of a separate Print Preview command in the File menu, your selected notes display automatically when you choose Print. The Print dialog box automatically previews your notes and you can page through the selected notes right there before you print.

Choosing Preview Orientation

By default your notes appear in portrait orientation, which is the 8.5-by-11-inch vertical format in which most traditional correspondence is printed. If you choose, you can change the page orientation to landscape orientation, so that the page prints in 11-by-8.5–inch mode.

1. In the Preview window, click the Landscape option to display the note in landscape orientation.

2. If you want to change back to Portrait orientation, click the Portrait option.

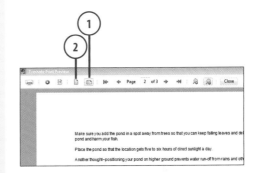

Choose Your Orientation

Landscape orientation can be handy when you have large graphics, tablets, or web clippings that take up the majority of the width of a traditional page.

Paging Through Your Note

The Page controls in Print Preview enable you to move page by page through the previewed notes. You can also jump to the beginning or end of the notes if you like.

1. Click Next Page to display the next page of your note.

2. Click Previous Page to move back through your notes.

3. Click in the text box and type a page number to move to a specific note.

4. Click Last Page to jump to the last page of the selected notes.

5. Click First Page to move to the first page in the selected notes.

Selecting Notes to Preview

You can change the notes displayed in the Preview window by selecting a different range of notes in the Evernote window.

Zooming and Reducing Note Display

The Zoom In and Zoom Out tools in Print Preview enable you to move in closer to the previewed note or—you guessed it—zoom out to see the full page.

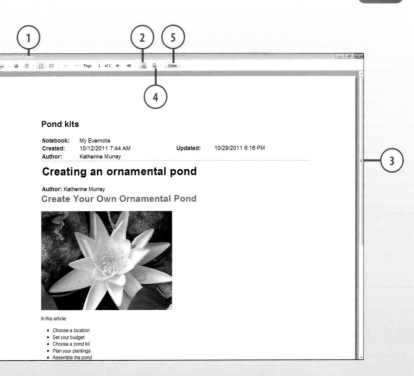

1. Select the notes you want to preview and Choose File, Print Preview.

2. If you want to zoom in on the current note, click Zoom In.

3. Use the vertical scroll bar to scroll down through the document.

4. Click Zoom Out to display the full note page.

5. When you're ready to close Print Preview, click Close.

It's Not All Good

Funky Close-Ups

The Zoom In and Zoom Out tools in Print Preview aren't all they're cracked up to be. You'll first experience a little oddness when you click Landscape Orientation. The page zooms up and magnifies in the Preview window, and you'll need to scroll through the note to see the full content.

When you click Zoom In or Zoom Out, you will discover that each setting changes the display only one increment, so both views are limited. If you Zoom Out to full-page view, you'll be able to see the entire note on one page, but if you click Zoom In, the page zooms to a great degree. Perhaps a future Evernote version will provide incremental zoom tools that enable us to choose from among different increments as we magnify and reduce the note display.

Printing Notes and Notebooks

After you've previewed your content and you're ready to print your note, you can make a few more choices about what you want to include with the note printout, and how—and where—you want to print it.

Setting Printing Options

When you choose to print your notes, you begin in the Print dialog box. You can choose your printer, and specify the number of copies you want to print.

1. Click File to display the File menu.

2. Click Print. The Print dialog box appears.

3. Click the printer you want to use to print the notes.

4. Click the number of copies you want to print.

5. Click Print.

Choosing Printer Preferences

In the Print dialog box, click the Preferences button to display options that are specific to the type of printer you have installed for your Windows computer.

Setting Print Attributes

The Print Options enable you to choose how each note is printed (the default is that each note is printed on a separate page) as well as choose the note attributes that are printed with the note selection.

1. Open the Print dialog box by selecting Print from the File menu or by pressing Ctrl+P.

2. Click the Options button.

3. If you don't want notes to print on different pages, click to clear the check box.

4. Click to add or remove any of the attributes you want to leave off of or include on the notes you print.

5. Click OK.

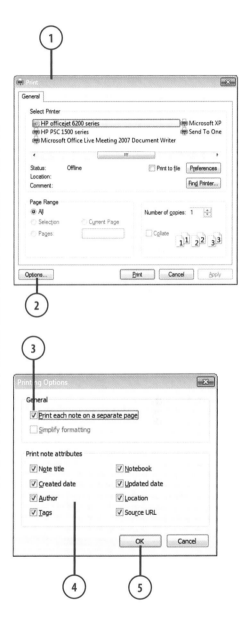

Printing Your Note

When you're ready to print the selected notes, you can click the Print tool in the Print Preview window or click File to open the File menu and click Print. You can then choose the remaining print options and send the notes to your printer. Begin by turning on your printer and making sure the printer is loaded and ready to print.

1. Open the Print dialog box by selecting Print from the File menu or by pressing Ctrl+P.

2. Click the printer you want to use.

3. Click the number of copies you want to print.

4. Click Print. The selected notes are sent to the printer.

Printing to a File

You can also choose to print your notes to a file, and Evernote will display the Save As dialog box. You can choose the folder in which you want to save the file, and Evernote will save the file as a PostScript file, which you can print easily later from any computer.

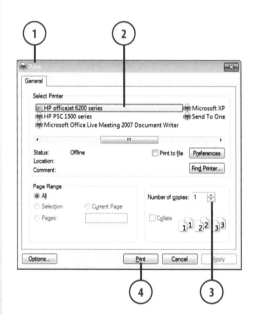

Printing to a PDF

Your Mac computer includes features built into the Print process in Evernote that enable you to print your notes directly to PDF files. This is handy if you want to create a non-editable version of your notes that you can circulate among friends and colleagues no matter what type of computer you use. Begin by choosing Print from the File menu.

1. Click File to display the File menu.

2. Click Print. The Print dialog box appears.

3. In the Print dialog box, preview the notes by paging through the preview using the buttons provided.

4. Click the PDF arrow.

5. Click the PDF option that reflects what you want to do. If you choose Save as PDF, Evernote displays a dialog box where you can enter a filename and click Save. If you click Save PDF to Evernote, the PDF is saved and added to a new Evernote note.

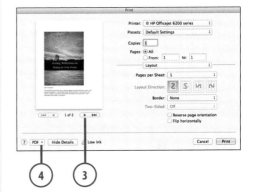

Share your Evernote notebooks
with individuals or your public

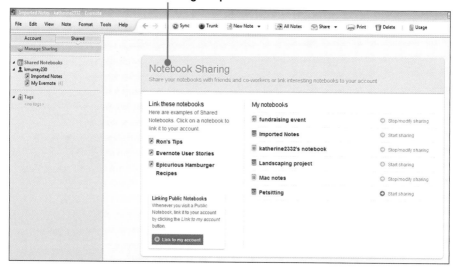

Tweet your notes

Share your
notes on
Facebook

You can easily share your notebook with a few friends or colleagues or with the world—on the web or through Twitter, email, or Facebook. In this chapter, you learn to share your notebooks by completing the following tasks:

→ Sharing a Public Notebook
→ Sharing Your Notebook with Individuals
→ Sharing Your Notes through Email and Social Media

Sharing Notes with Others

Many of the notebooks you create may be for your eyes only. Perhaps you're gathering information on how to build a new deck; you're planning a design for a new product; you are collecting research about a new program you would like to offer in the spring. But in some situations, you may want to create and maintain a shared notebook where several of you can capture your notes, review each other's thoughts, examine designs, and brainstorm new possibilities—all in the same shared notebook.

Evernote includes a number of sharing features you can use to share your notebooks with specific individuals or publicly, with the world. What's more, you can post your notes using Twitter, Facebook, or email, or you can copy and paste the URL of public notes into other places users can access them. Getting your thoughts out—while still making sure you have the privacy you want—is what this chapter is all about.

Your first task in sharing a notebook involves choosing the notebook you want to share and deciding how you want to share it. Evernote gives you two choices. You can share a notebook publicly—which means that anyone with the URL can view it—or you can share a notebook with specific individuals that you specify.

SHOULD YOU SHARE YOUR NOTEBOOK?

Different reasons exist for sharing your notebooks, and depending on the nature of the project you're working on, you may want to share the notebook publicly or send invitations to only a few people.

The way in which you will be able to work collaboratively in your notebook will depend on which Evernote version you use. If you are a free user, others will be able to only view the notes in your shared notebook—no editing allowed. If you are a premium account user, however, other users will be able to view, edit, and create notes in the shared notebook, whether they are premium users or not.

One big consideration when you create shared notebooks is how private the information needs to be. Publicly shared notebooks aren't secured, and any notes you share using social media—Twitter and Facebook, for example—can be picked up by search engines and so isn't secure. If you want to keep your information private in your shared notebook, give specific users the access they need to view (and edit) your notes. But remember that even those users can still copy the notes from your shared notebook if they like, so be sure to be explicit with your instructions if you want all that you've created to remain in the shared notebook.

Sharing a Public Notebook

Specifying a shared notebook as *public* in Evernote means that the notebook is given its own public URL address and anyone who has that address can view the notes in that notebook online. You might create a public notebook, for example, when you want to share information about an event you want to promote.

Sharing Your Notebook Publicly

When you share a notebook publicly, Evernote gives you the option of adding a notebook description and choosing how you want the notes in the notebook to be sorted and displayed.

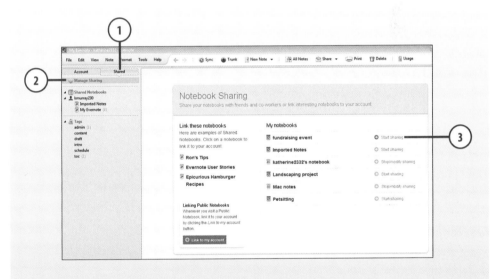

1. Click the Shared tab at the top of the left column in the Evernote window.

2. Click Manage Sharing.

3. In the Notebook Sharing window, click the Start Sharing link of the notebook you want to share.

4. In the Shared Notebook Settings window, click Start Sharing with the World.

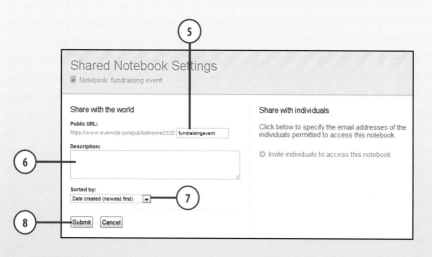

5. Click in the Public URL box if you want to change the name added at the end of the web address.

6. In the provided text box, type a description for the public notebook.

7. Click the Sorted By arrow to choose the order in which your notes will be sorted. You can choose to organize the notes by the date they were created, the date they were updated, or by title.

8. Click Submit to create the public notebook. Evernote displays the public URL others can use to view the notebook you've created.

Public URL Characters

For best results, avoid using characters such as spaces or special characters in the naming of your public notebook. Using one word or phrase (with no spaces) will help search engines and other users find you.

Where Will the Notebook Description Appear?

The notebook description you enter in the Shared Notebook Settings window appears at the top of the publicly shared notebook online. The description helps those viewing your notebook understand the overall scope of the notebook—just in case the individual note entries don't provide the information they need.

Accessing and Linking a Public Notebook

When you share the public link with someone else, she can access your shared notebook over the web. Here are the steps:

1. Open your web browser and enter the URL for the public notebook.

2. Evernote opens; review the note as needed.

3. If you want to add the note to your own notebook list, click the Link to My Account button.

4. In the screen that appears, click the Link This Notebook button.

You can share your notebook as
well by clicking Start Sharing.

5. If you want to return to viewing the public notebook, click View.

Don't Forget to Log In

If you haven't signed in to Evernote, you will be prompted to sign in before linking the public notebook to your account.

Sharing Your Notebook with Individuals

The notebooks that you share with individuals are more protected in that
only those you invite are able to see and share your notes. One drawback
here is that if you have a free account, other users can only view your notes
but not change them. If you have a premium account, however, users can
view and modify the notes in your shared notebook (no matter what kind of
account they have).

Go Further

WANT LOTS OF PREMIUM ACCOUNTS? THINK "SPONSOR"

Evernote has a plan that can help organizations—such as schools, nonprofit organizations, and businesses—get the best use of Evernote for the
money. By creating sponsored accounts for 25 or more users, you can con-
solidate billing, get priority support, and perhaps even get a discount.
Check out sponsored accounts at www.evernote.com/about/sponsor/.

Sharing with Individuals

The process for sharing a notebook with specific individuals involves sending an invitation by email that they can click and share your notebook. Yes, it's that easy.

1. Click the Shared tab at the top of the left column in the Evernote window.

2. Click Manage Sharing.

3. In the Notebook Sharing window, click the Start Sharing link of the notebook you want to share.

4. In the Shared Notebook Settings window, click Invite Individuals to Access This Notebook.

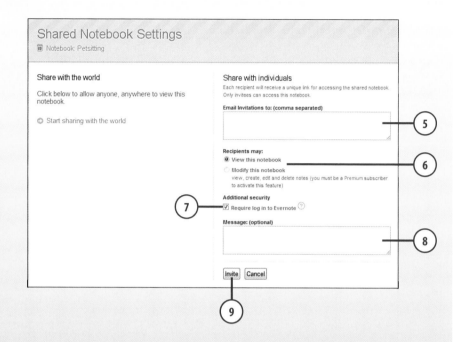

5. In the Email Invitations To field, type the email addresses of individuals you want to invite to share the notebook.

6. If you are using a premium account, you can choose whether you want those you invite to view or modify the notebook.

7. Under Additional Security, click the Evernote login option if you want to require users to log in to Evernote.

8. In the Message field, add a message to the people you're inviting to share the notebook.

9. Click Invite. The invitation is sent and Evernote lists the recipients of the invitation emails. If you are the recipient of an email invitation to a shared notebook, you can simply accept the invitation by clicking the link in the email message you receive.

Recognizing Shared Notebooks

You'll notice in the Notebooks list on the left side of the Evernote window that the small notebook icons change after you designate one or more as shared notebooks. By default, Evernote notebooks appear as small green notebook icons, but shared notebooks appear as little blue notebooks (and are those two small people on the front?). Whether your notebooks are shared with individuals or shared publicly, they have the same blue shared icon.

It's Not All Good

Sorry, Charlie—No Shared Searching

One feature that is lacking in Evernote in the shared notebook department is the ability to search across all shared notebooks. Suppose, for example, that you have created a number of shared notebooks that your team uses for a variety of purposes. You are preparing for a meeting and you are looking for a specific note about a new product that will be introduced in the spring—but where is it? Instead of doing one search that can pull up all results in your various notebooks (or using a saved search for this task), you have to go to each notebook and search the contents individually.

Yes, it's a pain, but Evernote developers say new-and-improved shared notebooks features are on the way, so check the Evernote site and forums for updates.

Another limitation to shared notebooks in Evernote is that you can't add a web clipping to one, even if all users have premium accounts. To add a web clipping to your shared notebook, first copy the web clipping to your own notebook (by right-clicking the selection in your web browser and clicking Add to Evernote 4.0, in Internet Explorer for example), and then copy the note to the shared notebook. Clunky, yes, but possible. Hopefully, this will be one of the limitations that will be addressed in future updates.

Copying To and From Shared Notebooks

You can easily copy notes to and from shared notebooks in Evernote. The process involves selecting the note (or notes) you want to copy, right-clicking, and selecting the notebook in which you want to save the note.

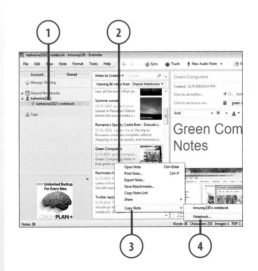

1. Click the notebook that contains the note you want to share.

2. Right-click the note.

3. In the context menu that appears, point to Copy Note.

4. Click Notebook. The Copy Note to Notebook dialog box opens.

5. Scroll through the list to find the notebook you want to copy the note to.

6. Click the notebook.

7. Click the option to save the dates the note was created and up-dated, if desired.

8. Click Preserve Tags if you want to copy the note tags.

9. Click Copy. The note is added to the notebook you specified.

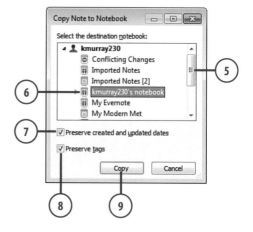

Where Did All the Tags Go?

Tags are a little odd in shared notebooks in Evernote. For one thing, you can see only the tags that are included in that specific notebook that's being shared. Next, you can only change the tags if you are the originator of the notebook. If you are a recipient—someone who has been invited to share the note-book—you'll be able to view but not modify or add tags.

Stop Sharing Your Notebook

If you want to change the sharing set-tings you've selected for your notebook, you can do so easily. You can modify your shared notebook settings at any time you are using Evernote.

1. In the Evernote window, click the Shared tab.

2. Click Manage Sharing.

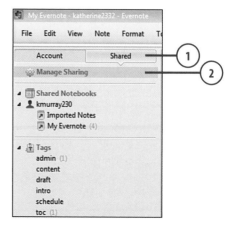

3. In the Notebook Sharing window, click the Stop/Modify Sharing link of the notebook you want to change.

4. In the Shared Notebook Settings window, click Stop Sharing. Evernote asks you to confirm your choice.

5. Click Yes. Evernote removes the shared setting.

Stopping Public Sharing

If you choose to stop sharing a notebook you've posted publicly, the process is the same: Click Manage Sharing, click the Stop/Modify Sharing link, and then click Stop Sharing. The only difference is that for public notebooks, you'll find the Stop Sharing link on the left side of the Evernote Shared Notebook Settings window.

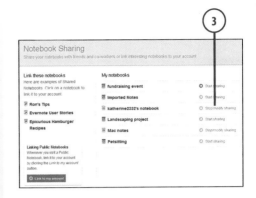

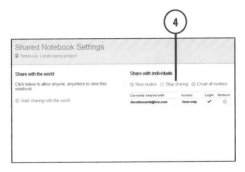

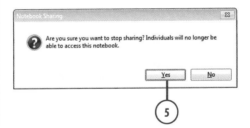

Sharing Your Notes Through Email and Social Media

If you're working on something you just can't resist sharing with your friends and fans, you can share your notes with social media right from your notebooks. Evernote makes it easy for you to share notes using your Twitter account, by sending them via e-mail, or by posting them to Facebook.

Sharing Notes Through Twitter

As you learned earlier in the book, you can easily set up Twitter so your tweets go directly to your Evernote account. You can also set up your notebook so that you can post directly to your Twitter feed as well. Pretty cool, eh?

1. Click the notebook containing the note you want to send.

2. Click the note in the notes list.

3. Click the Share arrow.

4. Click Post to Twitter. Evernote displays a web page where your note is converted to a tweet with the link to the shared note.

5. The Twitter page shows you the number of characters in your Evernote note. You can enter up to 140 characters of text. Click Tweet to share your post on Twitter.

Keeping It on the Down-Low

If you share a note using Twitter or Facebook, search engines will be able to see your content and your note may wind up in search results at some point. For that reason, if you want to keep something private you share with friends or followers, sending recipients a direct message might be better if you don't want the content to be visible in search results.

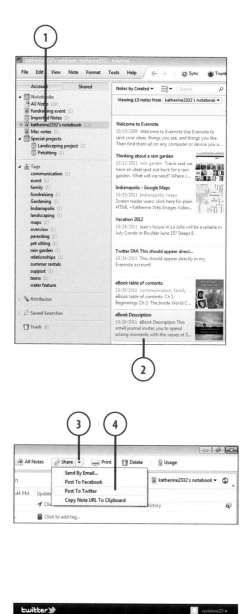

Sharing Your Notes with Facebook

If you've written something you want to share on Facebook, you can do that from your Evernote window.

1. Click the note you want to share on Facebook.

2. Click the Share arrow.

3. Click Post to Facebook. Evernote opens your web browser and displays the Post to Your Wall Facebook page.

4. Add a description if you like.

5. Click Share. The note is posted to your wall.

Facebook, Once and for All

Any notes you post from Evernote to Facebook will not update if you change the content of your note in your Evernote notebook. It's a one-time post that is actually placed on your Facebook page, which means the link to the note-book isn't maintained after you post the note content on Facebook.

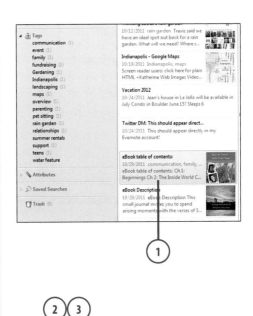

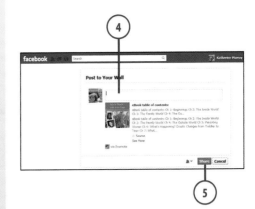

Sharing a Note by Email

You can easily send one or several notes by email, directly to a person in your address book. You'll find the Send By Email command in the Share tool at the top of the Evernote window.

1. Select the note or notes you want to share by email.

2. Click the Share arrow.

3. Click Send by Email.

4. In the To field, enter the email address of person you want to send the note to.

5. Change the Subject if you'd like.

6. Click the CC option to send yourself a copy of the email.

7. Add a description to send with the note.

8. Click Send.

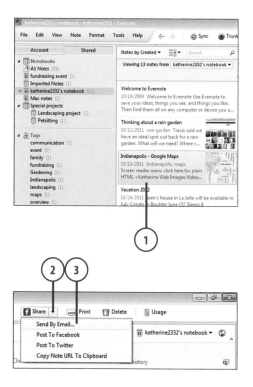

Copying a Note URL to the Clipboard

Another way to share notes in Evernote involves copying the note URL to your computer clipboard. After the note is on the clipboard, you can copy it to another place—for example, in a document or on a website—or you can share it through instant message with your favorite contacts. Simply select the note you want to share, click the Share arrow, and click Copy Note URL to Clipboard. Evernote places a copy of the URL on the clipboard so that you can paste it in other things.

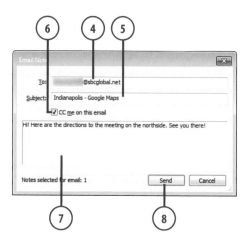

EMAILING YOUR TEAM

Go Further

>>>

You can use a command in Evernote to email all those sharing your notebook at one time. Suppose, for example, that you want to ask your team members to add all their ideas for the upcoming workshop by the end of the day on Friday so that you can all review the ideas at a meeting early next week. Click the Shared tab in the left panel of the Evernote window, and click Manage Sharing. Then, in the Notebook Sharing window, click the Stop/Modify Sharing link of the notebook you want to use.

When the Shared Notebook Settings window appears, click Email All Invitees, and Evernote opens your email program and starts a new email message, listing all your notebook team mates in the To line. You can fill in your message as you normally would, click Send, and the message goes out to all your shared notebook colleagues at once.

Index

Z

LIKE THIS BOOK? CHECK OUT OTHER TITLES IN THE SERIES

ISBN 13: 9780789748966   ISBN 13: 9780789748256   ISBN 13: 9780789749222   ISBN 13: 9780789748959

Full-Color, Step-by-Step Guides

The "My..." series is a visually rich, task-based series to help you get up and running with your new device and technology, and tap into some of the hidden, or less obvious, features. The organized, task-based format allows you to quickly and easily find exactly the task you want to accomplish, and then shows you how to achieve it with minimal text and plenty of visual cues.

Visit quepublishing.com/mybooks to learn more about the My... book series from Que.

quepublishing.com

My Evernote®

que

Katherine Murray

Safari
Books Online

FREE
Online Edition

Your purchase of *My Evernote* includes access to a free online edition for 45 days through the **Safari Books Online** subscription service. Nearly every Que book is available online through **Safari Books Online**, along with thousands of books and videos from publishers such as Addison-Wesley Professional, Cisco Press, Exam Cram, IBM Press, O'Reilly Media, Prentice Hall, Sams, and VMware Press.

Safari Books Online is a digital library providing searchable, on-demand access to thousands of technology, digital media, and professional development books and videos from leading publishers. With one monthly or yearly subscription price, you get unlimited access to learning tools and information on topics including mobile app and software development, tips and tricks on using your favorite gadgets, networking, project management, graphic design, and much more.

Activate your FREE Online Edition at
informit.com/safarifree

STEP 1:   Enter the coupon code: EGDZQZG.

STEP 2:   New Safari users, complete the brief registration form.
            Safari subscribers, just log in.

If you have difficulty registering on Safari or accessing the online edition,
please e-mail customer-service@safaribooksonline.com